basic
DIGITAL RECORDING

Printed by: MPG Books, Bodmin

Published by: Sanctuary Publishing Limited, Sanctuary House, 45-53 Sinclair Road, London
W14 0NS, United Kingdom. Web site: www.sanctuarypublishing.com

While the publishers have made every reasonable effort to trace the copyright owners for any or
all of the photographs in this book, there may be some omissions of credits for which we
apologise.

ISBN: 1-86074-269-6

basic
DIGITAL RECORDING

PAUL WHITE

Also by Paul White from Sanctuary Publishing

Also in this series

contents

chapter 2

chapter 3

....

chapter 4

....

chapter 5

chapter 6

introduction

Today the majority of recording systems are digital, but unlike in the era of analogue tape there's no longer a single accepted approach. Instead we are faced with a variety of technologies, some using tape, some using computer hard disk drives and some using MiniDiscs. Most of the cheaper systems are used with the computer desktop, on which digital recording is often combined with MIDI sequencing, but there are also stand-alone hard-disk recorders and digital tape recorders available. The type you choose will depend largely on the type of recording you wish to make and on whether or not you need to edit your recordings afterwards. The aim of this book is to explain the theory of digital recording and to discuss the various types of recording system currently on the market so that you'll be in a better position to decide which system is right for you. There are also numerous tips on how to keep computer-based systems working at maximum efficiency, along with some guidelines on recording and mixing.

20-bit or even 24-bit sampling. A 24-bit system samples with more than 16 million steps, which makes the 256 steps used by eight-bit sampling look a little inadequate!

Each bit used in a conventional sampling yields a maximum dynamic range of 6dB, so at best an eight-bit system can only provide a dynamic range of 48dB, which is about as noisy as a cheap cassette recorder. 16 bits, on the other hand, provides a maximum dynamic range of 96dB, which for most audio purposes is more than adequate, and even though 20- and 24-bit systems aren't yet perfected, they can still provide practical dynamic ranges in excess of 120dB.

sample rates

Although the minimum sample rate for serious audio work is 44.1kHz, less critical work is sometimes carried out at 32kHz (which reduces the audio bandwidth to under 15kHz). Most broadcasters prefer to work with a sample rate of 48kHz. Most DAT machines and soundcards support sample rates of both 44.1kHz and 48kHz, but it's important to note that everything else in the system must be set to run at the same sample rate, or the final audio recording will not play back at the same speed as that at which you recorded it. If you're planning on making CDs then you should always work at 44.1kHz, while if you're producing material for broadcasting you should stick to 48kHz.

Recent systems have been introduced that run at twice the current standard sampling rates, so now 88.2kHz and 96kHz can be added to the list. In theory these systems produce a slightly better sound quality, but in practice few people can detect a difference. Even so, it's important to be aware of them, especially as the 24-bit 96kHz audio used by DVD may become the standard hi-fi format.

sample rate converters

Sample rate conversion is necessary in those situations when you want to work at one sample rate but some of the source material is configured to another. It may be accomplished either with software or with an external hardware box, which will take in a digital signal at one sample rate and output it at another in real time.

To recap, then: systems with higher sampling frequencies can handle higher input frequencies, which in turn means a better frequency response. The only trade-off is that, because you end up recording a higher number of samples per second, more memory is needed to store the extra sound data. The same is true when recording more bits per sample. (The number of bits per sample is sometimes known as bit depth.) Fortunately, RAM (Random Access Memory) and computer hard drives are orders of magnitude cheaper now than they were a few years ago, so data storage is no longer the major cost concern it once was.

digital connections

Unlike analogue systems, on which every signal needs to be sent down a separate cable, digital systems allow two or more signals to be sent along the same cable while remaining completely separate. It's not important to know the theory behind this apparent magic at this stage, but it's important to know what is meant by the terms 'clocking' and 'sync'.

Let's say that you have a computer studio setup with a digital input and you want to transfer some music from a DAT (Digital Audio Tape) recorder into your computer, so the material enters the digital domain. The digital output from your DAT machine (probably an S/PDIF) phono connector must first be connected to the digital input of your computer interface or soundcard. S/PDIF is a standard connection protocol developed by Sony and Philips to be used with consumer digital equipment, and on some it may be provided as an optical port, as an alternative – or in addition – to a phono co-ax connector.

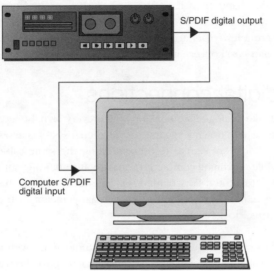

Figure 1.2: Digital connections
(S/PDIF with sync)

DAT machine (master)

S/PDIF digital output

Computer S/PDIF
digital input

Computer soundcard set to External Digital Sync mode

There are commercial-format adaptors available which
convert co-axial S/PDIF to optical, and vice versa.

This is where clocking comes in. When the DAT machine
is played, a highly accurate crystal clock controls the rate
at which the samples of data are played back to make sure
that the material is the same length and at the same pitch

as the original. To feed these little slices of data into a computer, the computer's sampling clock must be running at exactly the same rate as that of the DAT machine, but if the DAT machine and the computer are allowed to run independently, their clocks will always run at slightly different speeds, even if they're both set to the same frequency. This produces clicks and crackles in the audio as the two clocks drift in and out of sync.

clock sync

Fortunately, the digital data carried along an S/PDIF cable also carries the clock signal from the first machine, and this is used to sync the clock in the receiving device. However, the receiving device usually has to be set to Digital Sync mode for this to happen (see Figure 1.2). DAT machines without a word clock input facility switch to Digital Sync mode automatically if they are switched to digital input, which is sensible because there are no normal circumstances in which you'd want to accept a digital input while the receiving DAT machine was running from its own internal clock (Internal Sync mode). Nevertheless, some computer systems require you to select Digital Sync mode manually. The rule is that the source device runs from its own clock (Internal Sync mode) and the receiving device is set to Digital Sync mode. A number of devices can be cascaded in this way, but stringing more than four digital devices together in a chain may cause problems if the clock signal is corrupted.

Note, however, that more professional equipment is based on the AES/EBU digital interface, which can usually be identified by the presence of XLR connectors instead of phonos. In any event, the sockets are normally marked clearly on the rear panels of the equipment. Both S/PDIF and AES/EBU systems carry a stereo signal and a clock, but they operate at slightly different levels and so are not strictly speaking compatible (even though it's sometimes possible to use an adaptor lead to connect the two). AES/EBU is a balanced system and can use conventional mic cables over short distances, while S/PDIF is an unbalanced 70ohm system that requires proper digital 70ohm co-axial cable to work properly. You may be able to use audio phono leads over very short distances, but this isn't recommended because, although everything may seem to work fine, it may produce the occasional click in the audio stream.

word clock

Most professional systems have a word clock facility, which simply means that the sample clock is fed via separate sockets rather than being forced to rely on the clock embedded in the digital audio signal. In complex setups, this can be more accurate and less prone to clock corruption or problems involving jittery timing. Word clock usually travels via unbalanced cables capped with bayonet-fitting BNC connectors, and like other digital cabling it should be clearly labelled on the rear panel of the equipment. As with other digital clocking systems, there can only be one master – all the other pieces of equipment act as slaves, locking to the master clock. In large studios the word clock may come from a separate, high-accuracy clock generator with multiple outputs, synchronising everything in the studio, but in a project studio system it's more likely to originate from the digital console, if there is one. It's also common for systems to include a mixture, where some devices are locked to a master word clock while others (usually without a word clock input) are sync'ed via S/PDIF or AES/EBU.

digital effects

In the modern studio, digital electronics are used to record, process and mix sound. Effects and signal processors play a large role in contemporary music production, and now that digital circuitry can do virtually everything that analogue circuitry can, most hardware processing boxes have software equivalents that are available as plug-ins for the main audio software. Most studio effects are based on delay (echo, reverb, flanging, chorus and so on) or on pitch shifting. Processors, however, such as equalisers, compressors and gates, are more concerned with the dynamics of a signal. An overview of these basic effects follows.

digital reverberation

Reverberation occurs naturally when sound is reflected and re-reflected from surfaces within a large room, and an electronic reverb unit mimics this effect by electronically generating thousands of reflections. Reverb, like all modern effects, can be used to create the impression of sounds being recorded in a room, but it may also be used to create new effects that have no obvious counterpart in nature. Sounds produced in different types of rooms and with different materials acquire different qualities, which is why modern reverberation units provide a number of room types and user-adjustable parameters.

Most applications require a fairly short reverb time of between one and three seconds, although digital reverbs can also emulate caverns with decay times of ten seconds or even more. Plate settings are popular for general use, especially on vocals and drums. The term refers to the mechanical reverb plate that was used before digital reverb units were invented. In real life, each ear picks up a different pattern of reverb reflections, providing the brain with stereo information. Digital reverb units process a mono input to produce two different sets of synthetic reflections in order to create a convincing stereo effect. Figure 1.3 shows the pattern of decaying reflections created by a typical digital reverberation unit.

Good digital reverbs can produce excellent approximations of sounds being generated in real acoustic spaces, but they also have the capacity to create reverberant characteristics that simply couldn't occur in nature. Digital systems also allow us to produce reverb that is longer and brighter than anything normally encountered in nature.

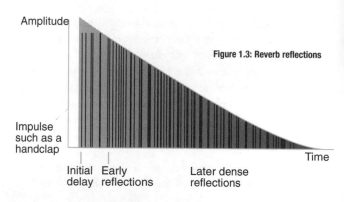

Figure 1.3: Reverb reflections

reverb parameters

The main reverb parameters available for user control are: pre-delay time, pattern and level of early reflection, overall decay time and high-frequency damping. Pre-delay simply determines the time between the original sound and the first reflection, and can be anything from virtually instantaneous to half a second or more.

Early reflection patterns are not usually variable. Normally the user can only select from a handful of stored patterns simulating various rooms, halls, chambers, plates or small-room ambience, although in some cases the level and spacing of these reflections can be altered. The impression of room size is increased if the reflections are spaced further apart.

Overall decay time simply determines the time it takes for the reverb to die away. Longer reverb times are suggestive of large environments with highly reflective surfaces, while shorter times may be used to simulate the natural acoustics of an average small room. Most reverb units can produce an impressively long decay time, but the most accurate way of judging the quality of a reverberator is to hear how convincingly it emulates small-room ambience.

The use of high-frequency damping means that the high-frequency decay time can be shorter than the overall decay time, and can therefore be used to simulate the absorbency characteristics of real rooms, simulating the way in which both surface and air absorption affect sound. Some units also have independent control over low-frequency damping, and can simulate environments that reflect mainly high-frequency sounds.

By selecting the right pattern for the environment you wish to simulate and then adjusting other parameters, the available effects can vary from a barely reverberant room to a huge hall where the reverb decay thunders on for several tens of seconds. In practice, because long reverbs tend to muddy a mix, most of the useful treatments have a decay time below two seconds, although there are occasions on which a long reverb can be effective.

Some models incorporate a control which determines the room size of the reverb by simultaneously adjusting several parameters to provide the impression of sounds occurring in a larger or smaller space. This is a useful control to have, as it saves time and means that you don't have to manually reprogram a number of parameters.

gated reverb

As well as the simulation of natural reverberation, two more effects have become standard issue in the modern digital reverb unit: gated reverb and reverse reverb.

Gated reverb was first created by using the (often heavily-compressed) ambience of a live room and a noise gate to produce an abrupt cutoff point rather than a smooth decay. Most reverb units provide an electronic emulation of this effect, using a burst of closely-spaced reflections that stop abruptly after around half a second.

Reverse reverb doesn't involve playing anything backwards, as the name might suggest, but is instead achieved by applying a reverse envelope to a group of reflections so that, instead of decaying, they increase in level after the original sound before cutting off. Like gated reverb, the most important parameter in this case is the time it takes for the reverb to build up and cut off.

delay and echo

A delayed sound is produced by delaying an audio signal in order to produce one or more distinct echoes. This is the electronic equivalent of a tape echo unit. A feedback or regeneration control adjusts the amount of output signal fed back into the input so that repeating echoes can be produced. To set up a single delay, the modulation depth, rate and feedback controls should be at their minimum settings, and the decay time may then be set as desired. To convert this single repeat into a true repeating echo is simply a matter of advancing the feedback control so that whatever appears at the output is then fed back to the input, returning and forming a delay loop. The feedback control determines the time it takes for the echoes to die away.

Modern multi-effects units often include multitapped delay programs, which generate a number of echoes set at different delay times. With these devices it may also be possible to pan the individual delays from left to right in the stereo field to create interesting spatial effects.

modulated delay

Originally conceived as the successors of tape loop echo machines, delay devices (and their software counterparts) soon acquired modulation controls that allowed them to produce a wide range of effects, from echo and doubling to chorus, flanging, ADT, vibrato and phasing. Indeed, many of the standard studio effects are variations on the theme of digital delay, where the delay time is modulated by an LFO (Low-Frequency Oscillator) to produce effects such as chorus, flanging, phasing and vibrato.

chorus and ADT

Chorus uses a short delay of up to about 70ms to create a slight doubling effect, and the delay time is then modulated to produce a slight wavering in pitch. An equal mix of the delayed and unprocessed sound is used to produce an interesting effect, which sounds rather like two instruments playing the same part but with slight differences in timing and tuning.

ADT (Automatic Double Tracking) is similar to chorus but uses a delay time in excess of 70ms to create a more pronounced doubling or 'slapback' effect, and the depth of modulation is shallower. ADT is often used to process vocals in order to obtain a thicker sound, making it sound like a singer has performed the same part twice, on different tape tracks. The amount of modulation should be so slight that it's only just noticeable.

flanging

Flanging is essentially similar to phasing, although it may use slightly longer delay times – up to 50ms, for instance – and the feedback control is advanced to produce a dramatic, swirling effect. In general terms, it's possible to get away with using more depth by using a slower modulation rate. The sound becomes more 'whooshy' if more feedback is applied.

phasing

Phasing uses shorter delay times than flanging, and little or no feedback, to produce a moving comb filter which sounds similar to mild flanging. Because the effect is more subtle, however, it can be used more extensively. A lot of music recorded in the Seventies features phasing on the lead guitar part.

vibrato

Vibrato is a modulation of pitch similar to that produced manually by a guitar or violin, and is created by using only the delayed sound and none of the original. The delay is kept to just a few milliseconds so that the timing of the performance isn't significantly affected, and the depth of modulation determines the depth of vibrato.

pitch shifting

Pitch shifters can change the pitch of the original signal without changing the speed of the sound, and they usually have a maximum range of at least an octave above and below the original sound. Most budget pitch shifters impart a strange timbre, which is caused by the regular modulation of the looping processes, but this side-effect can be disguised by mixing it with the original sound. There's also a slight delay due to the looping process, but this can be as short as just a few milliseconds. Smaller pitch shifts sound very similar to chorus, albeit without the chorus effect's regular modulation. Such detuning treatments – combined with a short delay – are also often used to double or thicken vocals.

autopanners

Autopanners are devices that automatically pan mono signals from left to right in the mix, usually under the control of a LFO or an external trigger. Used in time with the tempo of a track, panning can be applied quite subtly.

amp/speaker simulators

While keyboards usually work best when played through a sound system with a flat frequency response and minimal distortion, guitar and bass amplifiers are voiced, which means that their frequency response is shaped to suit the instrument rather than left flat. Furthermore, the loudspeakers and enclosures used in guitar and bass amplification usually have a very limited frequency response, which enables them to filter out the rougher-sounding components of amplifier distortion. If you were to DI (Direct Inject) a distorted guitar without EQ, the result would be a much thinner and more raspy version of what you would hear from an amplifier. To make DI'ing the guitar a more practical proposition, the amp/speaker simulator was devised. This device operates by using a filter circuit to mimic the amplifier and loudspeaker voicing of a typical guitar amplifier. Many multi-effects units now include amp/speaker simulators as well as overdrive, which enables the user to create a fully produced guitar sound with only one unit. The output may then be recorded without further processing.

filters

Effects units often include filters, not only in the form of parametric and graphic EQ but also as emulations of the swept-resonant filters used in synthesisers. The filter used in a typical analogue synthesiser is closely related to the parametric equaliser – the main difference is that the frequency of the filter can be controlled electronically rather left to the user. For example, an LFO could be used to sweep the frequency up and down, or an envelope could be generated to provide a filter sweep. Also, the filter can often be set to a higher Q (resonance) value – some can be set so high that they self-resonate and turn into an oscillator. Some of the more sophisticated multi-effects processors include not only resonant synth-type filters but also a variety of possible control sources, including envelopes derived from the input signal level, MIDI-triggered envelopes, LFOs and so on.

MIDI control

MIDI-plus-audio sequencers can use MIDI information to automate certain effects parameters (as long as the machine is equipped with a MIDI control facility), and it's also possible for many plug-in effects to be automated.

All but the very cheapest digital effects units are now programmable, offering MIDI control over patch selection as well as some form of dynamic MIDI control over effect parameters. The ability to program effects enables the user to set up several effects of each type, and with chorus, flanging, ADT, vibrato and other DDL-based effects, these programs, once created, can be used in a number of different contexts with little or no further modification. If there are more than 128 presets and user patches, these are normally organised into banks so that they can be accessed using MIDI Bank Change messages.

patching effects

Effects such as reverb are normally fed from a post-fade (effects) send control, which means that, if the channel fader is moved, the reverb level will increase and decrease along with the original sound. This is obviously the way you'd normally want to work, although it's possible to drive a reverb unit from a pre-fade send if you want to fade out the dry (uneffected) signal while still leaving the reverb audible. This procedure is useful in producing unusual or special effects.

The aux send system has the advantage that it allows the same effects device to be shared among all of the mixer channels while still allowing the user to have different amounts of effect on each channel. For example, you might be able to use the same reverb setting on both drums and vocals, but you may want to use more on the vocals than on the drums.

processors

Examples of processors include exciters, equalisers, compressors, limiters, gates, expanders and autopanners. All of these devices change either the level or the tonal quality of the signal passing through them, and you wouldn't normally add a dry signal to the output of one of these units. Because aux sends are used to add the output from an effect to the dry signal, it isn't common practice to connect a processor via an aux send; instead they are connected by an insert point – usually into a mixer channel or group. Most of these processors were originally designed to be analogue, and so will be described as such where appropriate. However, they are all available in digital versions in both hardware and software form.

compressors/limiters

Compressors are used to even out excessive peaks in signal level that occur in vocal or instrumental performances, and they do this by changing the gain of the signal path depending on the level of the signal passing through. Just as an engineer might pull down a fader if the level gets too high, a compressor will lower the level if it exceeds a threshold set by the user, so that signals falling below the threshold level remain unchanged. The degree of gain reduction applied is set by the compression ratio control setting, as shown in the graph in Figure 1.4.

When the ratio is very high, the compressor's maximum output is maintained at the threshold level and is effectively prevented from going beyond it. This imposes a limit on the maximum signal level, regardless of the input, and a compressor used with a high ratio setting is often described as a limiter, hence the term compressor/limiter. As a rule, high compression ratios are used in conjunction with high threshold settings, so that only the signal peaks are affected. Lower ratios may be used with lower threshold settings to provide gain levelling over a greater dynamic range.

The compressor's attack control determines how quickly the circuitry responds to a signal once it has

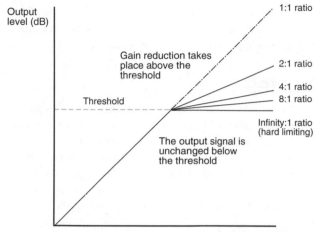

Figure 1.4: Compressor graph

exceeded the threshold, while the release control determines the time it takes for the gain to return to normal once the input has dropped back below the threshold. Most two-channel compressors have a Stereo Link switch so that stereo signals can be processed. In Stereo Link mode both channels are compressed by the same amount, thus preventing the image from appearing to move to one side or the other when a loud sound appears on only one side of the mix.

Limiting is used in those circumstances when it would be undesirable for a signal to exceed a specific level – to prevent clipping on a digital recorder, for example.

gates

Whereas compressors control the levels of signals that exceed a threshold, gates control the levels of signals which fall below a threshold. The aim is to silence the signal during pauses, when background noise isn't masked by a signal. If the gate's threshold is set at a level just above the background noise, the gate will operate whenever there is a pause in the signal.

Gates are used to mute spill from other instruments as well as to tackle straightforward noise or hiss, and they are used regularly in the miking of drum kits – for example, in preventing the bass drum mic from picking up the other drums in the kit. They are also often used with electric guitars, combating the high levels of noise and hum generated by guitar amplifiers when the guitarist is not actually playing. Vocals may also be gated to hide the sounds of rustling clothing and breathing.

It must be understood that gates only remove noise when there is a pause in the wanted signal – they can't help with noise that's audible over the top of the

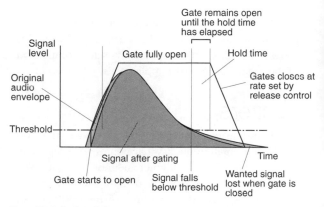

Figure 1.5: Operation of a gate

programme material. Figure 1.5 describes a gate's reaction when the signal falls below the threshold level. Expanders are very similar to gates, except that they close down gently, more like a compressor in reverse.

equalisers

Equalisers are essentially tone controls. Most mixers are equipped with built-in EQ, but it's often useful to have a high-quality external equaliser (or its software counterpart) that can be patched in via an insert point for those occasions when more precise control is required. Parametric equalisers are the most versatile, but they also take a long time to set up properly. The book *basic EFFECTS AND PROCESSORS* – also in this series – provides and in-depth analysis and comparison of these devices and their applications.

exciters

Also known as enhancers, exciters are devices that add synthesised high-frequency harmonics to a signal in order to make it sound brighter and more intimate. The process, which was developed and patented by the company Aphex, is different to the process of equalisation, which can only redistribute those harmonics that already exist. Exciters are used to push sounds to the front of a mix, or to create an impression of clarity and space in crowded mixes. They can be used on both entire mixes and individual tracks, and may also be used to brighten stereo mixes which are destined to become masters, for the mass-copying of cassettes, in order to compensate for the loss of high-frequency sounds that cassette duplication often entails. Enhancers working on slightly different principles are available from other manufacturers.

recording systems

Only a few short years ago tapeless recording was too expensive to contemplate, but now the cost of the hardware involved has come in down in price so much that it is now the least costly of all of the options available. However, hard-disk recording is accompanied with its own set of choices and challenges – for example, which computer should you choose? And if you prefer to use hardware, which company provides the best equipment for your requirements?

Should you decide to use a computer recording system, it's possible to record audio onto a Macintosh with nothing more than the appropriate software (audio inputs and outputs are built into all current models), or you can record onto a PC fitted with a suitable soundcard and software. Alternatively, you can use a computer with additional external hardware (such as Digidesign's ProTools III), thus relieving the computer of most of the burden of processing and mixing audio.

If you prefer to use hardware, however, there are stand-alone, hard-disk-based digital workstations available which offer upwards of eight tracks, and many of these machines cost little more than their obsolete analogue-cassette-based counterparts. Prices have fallen significantly because, unlike analogue recording, the hardware used in tapeless systems is based on the same components that are used elsewhere in the computer industry, which means that the economics of scale are, for once, on the side of the consumer.

audio quality

16-bit hard-disk recording can provide the same quality of audio reproduction as a CD, but it's not always wise to take that level of performance for granted because the quality of the fidelity is also limited by the quality of the analogue-to-digital converters, and indeed to how they are used. For example, high-quality converters in an external rack box are likely to sound every bit as good as a CD, while budget converters housed in a computer – either as part of the basic hardware or on a cheap soundcard – are more likely to pick up some noise from the computer's own electronic components. They may also use budget converter chips, which offer relatively poor resolution and cause increased noise and distortion. Most professional hardware can now work at 16- or 24-bit resolution, and support for the 96kHz sampling rate is becoming commonplace, but a well-designed 16-bit system that can run at either 44.1kHz or 48kHz is more than adequate for most applications. Ultimately, the CD format is limited to 16-bit, 44.1kHz resolution – and you know how professional a well-recorded CD can sound!

input/output

Input/output (or I/O for short) describes both the analogue and digital inputs and outputs of an audio system. The amount of I/O you need depends on your working methods – if you only ever record one part at a time and intend to handle everything with the computer then you may need nothing more than a stereo in/stereo out card. On the other hand, if you plan to use an external mixer you may need a system with eight or more discrete analogue outputs, and if you're looking to record several parts at the same time you'll need a card with multiple analogue inputs.

Users with digital mixers or digital tape machines may benefit from a system that offers A-DAT lightpipe compatibility, which allows eight channels of digital audio to be transferred along a single fibre-optic link. In any event, it's usually wise to choose a card that has stereo digital ins and outs (usually S/PDIF) so that it's possible to record information to and from formats such as DAT, CD/CD-R or MiniDisc. As you'd expect, systems with more I/O capabilities are more expensive, so think carefully about your current and future needs before deciding on which system you're likely to need.

random access

The advantage that hard-disk recording has over tape recording is that computer hard drives can reach any piece of data within a few milliseconds – you don't need to wait for a tape to wind to your chosen location. This attribute is known as random access (unlike the linear medium used by tape-based systems).

Modem AV drives are equipped with intelligent thermal recalibration systems which avoid interrupting when the disk is reading or writing data, making them a better choice for multitrack work. Virtually all modern hard drives are AV compatible, you should be careful if you find an old drive in the cupboard that you think might be useful. As a rule, EIDE drives (Enhanced Integrated Drive Electronics), which are used inside most Macs and PCs currently on the market, are slower than SCSI drive (Small Computer System Interface – pronounced 'scuzzi'), although there are also several variations of SCSI available, with SCSI II being logically faster than SCSI I. Future systems are likely to rely on the Firewire connection protocol, which is significantly faster than SCSI, in which case the ultimate limitation is that of the speed of the drive mechanism itself. Even so, a cheap EIDE drive should let you play back at least eight tracks of 16-bit, 44.1kHz audio simultaneously.

non-destructive editing

Because random access allows you to call up any piece of data almost instantly, you can rearrange the sections of your recording and play them back in any order. Rearranging, copying and removing material without in any way affecting the original is known as non-destructive editing, and there's a lot that can be done to a recording without the original data changing in any way. Even so, there are times when it may be desirable for a change to be permanent – for example, when silencing noise immediately before the start of a song, or when changing the actual level of the recorded audio. This type of edit is destructive, because the original data has been changed.

editing features

The most effective editing tricks available for digital systems are based around the rearranging of material into a different order, although it's also possible to normalise signal levels, bring peaks up to 0dB, apply digital EQ, reverse sections of sound, create fade-ins and fade-outs, and a number of other functions which would have been difficult or impossible on a tape system, whether digital or analogue. Most systems are now capable of supporting software-based plug-in effects, such as reverb, delay, compression and stereo enhancement. However, before I get too enthusiastic, it's only fair that I should warn you of the disadvantages of recording to disk.

hard-disk limitations

Over half an hour of eight-track audio can be recorded onto onto a cheap VHS video tape, but even with the falling cost of hard drives it would still cost you a lot more than the price of one of these if you wanted to leave the recording on the drive once you'd finished it. There are removable disk systems available which can store data on removable cartridges with capacities of a couple of gigabytes or more, but they still cost significantly more than tape-based systems on a per-track-minute basis. With recording time, it's a general rule that one track-minute of 14-bit, 48kHz audio eats up around 5Mb of memory.

Because hard drives aren't yet cheap enough to use for permanent archiving (in a project studio environment, at least), some form of backup system is needed. CD-R (Recordable Compact Disc) is good for storing up to around two track-hours of audio, and for those who need a greater capacity, writable DVD (Digital Versatile Disc) is becoming cheaper all the time. Many professionals still favour the Exobyte tape backup systems used by the computer industry. Backing up material onto digital tape is obviously quite slow, but the relative cheapness of the equipment often makes it worth the inconvenience.

It's important to make backups because, if a disk becomes corrupted after a computer crash, all data could be lost. If a section of tape becomes damaged, however, the rest of the reel or cassette will still be playable.

what can a computer do?

Because computer audio technology is evolving at such a rate, you may not be aware of all the things of which a desktop music system is capable. Computers were first drafted into musical circles to handle MIDI sequencing, and then multitrack audio was added. The main benefit of a computer-based system is that digital audio can be integrated into MIDI sequencing packages; any recorded audio can be accessed and arranged in the same way as sequenced MIDI patterns are arranged. This means that you only have to pay for one computer to work on both, and you don't have to keep changing your mental outlook as you switch from MIDI to audio.

If you already work mainly with MIDI then adding a few tracks of hard-disk audio is a very practical and flexible way to upgrade, as it removes the need to synchronise a tape system to a MIDI sequencer. Because a typical MIDI composition may only include a small amount of audio (vocals and guitar parts, for example), removable drives become more cost effective as a storage medium. My own preference, however, is to complete an album on a conventional, fixed hard drive and then back up both the audio files and the MIDI data onto one or more CD-Rs.

Software mixing, EQ, signal processing and effects have now been brought into the computer domain, with effects and processors available as plug-ins. Plug-ins are separate pieces of software that can be added to your main audio program to increase its functionality. However, unlike most add-on software, the new functions appear from within your main audio program. For example, the widely adopted VST plug-in format set up by Steinberg allows the plug-ins to be used from within the digital mixing section of the software, usually via insert points in the channels or groups. Plug-ins are generally purchased separately, from third-party manufacturers with different specialities, but programs such as LogicAudio and Cubase VST come with some genuinely useful plug-ins to help you get started.

Note that Digidesign's ProTools system uses its own format of plug-in (TDM) because the plug-ins have to be written to run on their DSP (Digital Signal Processing) cards, rather than the host computer's processor. A few other systems exist that require a proprietary plug-in format, but VST has taken off as a standard for most audio/MIDI sequencers on both Mac and PC.

As the processing power of computers continues to increase, designers are never far behind in thinking up new, creative ways of using it. Software synthesisers have become popular in recent years, and some are surprisingly powerful, even though it's difficult to obtain the right software drivers. Steinberg's ASIO standard is widely supported, which means that the output from a synth can be sent via a regular soundcard. Software drivers are required whenever a piece of hardware needs to interface with a piece of software – it acts as a translator between the two. All soundcards need drivers, as do printers, CD-R recorders and external MIDI interfaces.

ReWire

To make it possible to use a synth at the same time as a sequencer, Steinberg (in conjunction with Propellerhead Software) have provided a solution in the form of ReWire, a system which allows these virtual synths to be routed inside any Mac or PC MIDI/audio sequencer that supports it. ReWire effectively allows a synth to be routed through the audio software's mixer section just like any other audio track, and it can handle up to 64 channels of real-time audio at once.

software samplers

There are currently a few software samplers on the market for both Mac and PC, and I envisage that software sampling and sample playback will be an area of significant growth over the next couple of years. We may even see sampling offered as a standard feature on MIDI sequencers before too long. When you consider that computers can already handle CD burning (writing material onto CD-Rs) quite easily, it should be of no surprise that a well-thought-out computer-based desktop system can handle a complete music project, from recording to CD mastering, without the need to use additional hardware other than mics, pre-amps and a monitoring system.

hard-disk editors

Hard-disk editors exist specifically to manipulate and rearrange stereo (or sometimes surround sound) material, and they are most commonly used to compile individual tracks in order to produce a production master tape for an album project, or to chop up and move the various sections of a song around in order to create a new arrangement. Such editing techniques are often used to create extended remixes or to shorten songs. Sophisticated crossfading algorithms are used to ensure that there are no audible glitches at the edit points – something that isn't always possible when editing analogue tape with razor blades! Hard-disk editing is also frequently used to assemble the best parts of several different takes of the same song into a composite piece.

While basic cut-and-paste editing is possible on a multitrack hard-disk system, a dedicated stereo-editing system or software package will usually include specialist tools that can be used to edit to a much finer degree. Like those in the mainstream multitrack packages, there are also third-party software plug-ins that provide functions such as compression, limiting, EQ, noise reduction, noise-shaped dithering, stereo-image correction and even three-dimensional sound processing. Most of the current editing packages also include the ability to burn audio CDs with a cheap CD-R recorder. If the CD-R is to be used as a master for duplication purposes, however, the software package must include the PQ encoding (Pause and Cue information) that is used in commercial CDs.

hard-drive practicalities

If you're running a hard-disk recording system on a computer, with or without external hardware, it's always better to use a separate drive to store your audio data. Unlike tape systems, hard drives record their information wherever they can find space, and if you're using the same disk for word processing, sorting your programs and handling your e-mail, the audio files could end up being spread all over the drive. This process is know as fragmentation, and the more fragmented your drive the slower it gets. Even if you're using a separate drive for sound editing, the fact that you're likely to keep adding recordings to it means that it will occasionally need to be defragmented, using specialist software such as Norton Utilities. This software moves all of the pieces of file data around so that the information is stored in contiguous sections of the drive.

A separate drive doesn't necessarily have to take the form of an external box, however; most computers have provision for the attachment of an extra internal drive. SCSI drives are often used for audio purposes because they're faster than the EIDE drives used inside PCs and Macs, but unless you need a lot of tracks an EIDE drive may well do the job at around a third of the price of its SCSI counterpart. It'll also save you the expense of buying a SCSI card for your computer.

If you find that you really need to use a large number of tracks, you should choose a fast SCSI Ultra II or SCSI Ultra III drive and a suitable SCSI interface card. As a rule, the faster the spindle speed of the drive (measured in rpm) the faster the drive's data transfer rate. You should look for a drive with a high rate of sustained transfer, not just a fast access time, and it's always wise to ask the manufacturer of your audio software if they can recommend specific drives. As a rule of thumb, 16 tracks of 16-bit, 44.1kHz audio require a disk with a sustained transfer rate of 1.4Mb per second, and even relatively slow drives can perform better than this. At the other end of the scale, a SCSI Ultra II drive may have a rate of sustained data transfer in excess of 50Mb per second.

Stereo material sampled at 44.1kHz (the same rate as CD sampling) uses around 10Mb of disk space per minute, which means that around 600Mb of disk space is required to hold an hour's worth of stereo material. In practice rather more is required because, if you decide to perform a destructive edit, the system usually creates backup files so that you can change your mind if things don't work out. In multitracking, the recording time is halved every time the number of tracks is doubled, so if you're using the same 600Mb drive you're looking at a 15 minutes of continuous eight-track recording or less than eight minutes of 16-track recording. It's also worth noting that larger-capacity drives are usually faster, making them more suitable for multitracking purposes. As prices of hard drives are now much cheaper than they used to be, it's a good idea to budget for a drive with at least twice as much capacity as you think you'll need.

recording hardware

The way in which the computer system records your audio material depends on the hardware; budget soundcards are usually equipped with only analogue inputs and outputs, while more sophisticated systems also have S/PDIF and/or AES/EBU digital interfaces. The input and output converters and connectors may be situated on the soundcard itself or mounted within an external box. External box-mounted systems allow more space in which to accommodate connectors, and also allow the converters to be mounted away from the electrically noisy environment of the computer.

Analogue recordings are fine for multitrack work because most of the source material is analogue (all you need to do is run line outs from a mixer or recording pre-amp), but when editing stereo material it's generally considered unacceptable to leave the digital domain unless you specifically need to process the audio signal with an analogue device, such as an esoteric equaliser, in which case the digital data which is to be edited is usually fed in from DAT via the digital I/O connectors. A tip here is to buy a proper digital transfer cable, which has a different impedance to that of audio cable; and while you may be able to get away with using a hi-fi phono lead, you might end up with unexplained clicks and glitches.

choosing a computer

When choosing a computer, you should first decide which software you want to run on it. If you're not sure, ask other people what they're using in their own systems. For MIDI/audio recording most people seem to use either Emagic's Logic Audio or Steinberg's VST, although in the USA packages such as MOTU's Digital Performer, Cakewalk and Opcode's StudioVision are also very popular. All of these packages offer sophisticated MIDI and audio recording and editing capabilities, so you should choose that which best suits your working methods. In some cases the choice of whether to use Mac or PC will be made for you, because the software will only run on one or the other, but some programs are available for both platforms, in which case you can still choose the computer you prefer.

Macintoshes are generally easier to set up and use than PCs, but they cost a little more and are not as easy to upgrade. Personally, I think that it's worth spending a little extra money on a Macintosh, but most people choose PCs because they're cheaper and more widespread. If you're buying Mac hardware you know exactly what you're getting, but PCs come from a variety of sources and not all models are equally well suited to music work. If you're contemplating buying a PC-based system I'd recommend that you buy the whole system from the same supplier. If you buy your package as a complete system from a single supplier, it's up to them to make sure that everything works so that they can't pass the buck onto another company. You may also get a larger discount if you buy everything from one source.

hardware recorders

Hardware hard-disk recorders are usually designed to function very much like tapeless tape recorders, although it's common for manufacturers to include some editing facilities that wouldn't be available on their system's tape counterpart. The most important benefit with hardware systems is that they work straight out of the box, and you don't have to worry about whether your computer, software, soundcard and hard drive are compatible. They also feature conventional metering, multiple inputs and outputs and gapless punching in and out, which works just as it would on a tape machine.

Computer-based systems, on the other hand, can suffer from a noticeable amount of monitoring latency, depending on the system. Latency is a very important subject and will be discussed later, but essentially it's a delay between the point at which a signal being fed into the system and its appearance at the system's monitor output. Latencies of several tens of milliseconds are common in cheaper systems, and such a delay can be enough to interfere with timing when overdubbing parts.

digital tape

Digital tape machines, such as the Alesis A-DAT and Tascam DA series, are simple to operate, with cheap media and a wide user base. These are both eight-track machines, but because they can be used in multiples they are known as MDMs (Modular Digital Multitracks).

Two or more MDMs can be locked together when more than eight tracks are needed, although the few seconds it takes for the machines to lock up each time can be frustrating when punching in and out. Little editing is possible, unfortunately, though if a suitable controller is used it's possible to offset one machine against another so that sections from one machine can copied onto different locations on the other. For example, you may want to copy the backing vocals from one verse onto all of the other verses – which is pretty much the extent of the editing that a tape-based system can perform, and even carrying out this simple task is much more time-consuming and cumbersome than it is on a computer.

Computer interfaces and software systems are available which allow audio to be transferred from a digital multitrack recorder onto a computer, edited, and then returned to any location on the multitrack recorder to single-sample accuracy. This is clearly useful in situations where tape is the most practical medium for recording (such as when recording large bands or location recording) but where some post-production work needs to be carried out later.

tapeless workstations

Hard-disk recording systems require DSP power to process data, and although modern computers are incredibly powerful there may still come a time when you need to exceed the computer's capabilities. The next logical step in this case is to add more DSP power to handle processor-intensive tasks such as digital mixing and real-time signal processing.

In developing their ProTools package, Digidesign have

adopted the approach of a computer-based workstation, fitting DSP cards inside the computer or in an expansion chassis. Using their TDM (Time Division Multiplex) buss, data can be routed around the system very quickly, making it possible to create a virtual recording and mixing environment. The system's only limitation is the amount of DSP power available to it. Other companies also offer hardware solutions, ranging from Yamaha's cheap SW1000XG synth/mixer/effects/ audio recording card up to immensely powerful packages which cost much more than the computer to which they are attached. Unless your requirements are especially demanding, however, a host-powered system based around a powerful computer should be able to cope with between 16 and 24 audio tracks, provide mixing with basic EQ and still have enough power left over to run a handful of plug-in effects.

The latest affordable hardware options are really the modern counterparts of the old cassette multitrackers, in that they provide eight or more recording tracks, along with digital mixing and effects. These systems often offer automated mixing features and the ability to generate MIDI timecode for synchronising to a sequencer, but their most popular feature is that they are a one-box solution to recording and mixing. With nothing more than a few mics and a monitoring system you can start work right away. Some systems can even burn material onto CDs, and because everything is in one box they're also useful for location recording. The negative side to most hardware systems, however, is that they don't always integrate with MIDI systems as smoothly as MIDI-plus-audio software, and most can't be expanded.

digital mixers

Although a computer is quite capable of mixing signals, it's sometimes useful to use a hardware mixer on which all of the controls can be accessed directly on the front panel, and on which levels can be controlled with physical faders. The benefit of using a traditional analogue mixer is its familiar format, with only one knob per function, and the low cost at which additional inputs and insert points can be added. The disadvantages are that the introduction of automation (beyond that of basic fader and mute automation) isn't particularly cost effective, and that every time a signal is bounced it has to be converted from digital to analogue and then back again.

On a digital system, incorporating a digital mixer means that signals can be kept in the digital domain (thus preserving signal quality), and most digital mixers provide the ability to automate EQ, pan and level, as well as aux send levels and even types of effect. On simpler systems the automation may be in snapshot form, where each snapshot comprises a series of console settings that can be switched in at the appropriate point in a song, although on more up-market models it's usual to have fully dynamic automation controlled via an internal automation system, on either an external computer or a MIDI sequencer. The majority of digital consoles also include effects such as reverb and delay as well as dynamic processing, such as gates and compression. This mitigates the lack of insert points to some extent, although it does restrict your options when you want to use external effects and processors.

The down side of using digital mixers is that it's seldom practical to provide one knob per function, and so the operating system is invariably less intuitive than that for an analogue mixer. Furthermore, additional analogue inputs, outputs and insert points require expensive A-to-D (Analogue-to-Digital) and D-to-A converters, and so cheaper models are likely to have quite limited analogue I/O facilities. Connection to computers or hardware digital recorders is likely to be via an A-DAT lightpipe or a similar multichannel digital interface, although newer and faster systems based on Firewire technology are likely emerge. In a small studio system where synchronisation is achieved via word clock, the mixer is likely to be used as the word clock source.

stereo recorders

Even though a lot of today's music is generated inside the computer, there's still a need for hardware stereo recorders such as DAT machines and MiniDisc recorders, both of which are available with digital and analogue ins and outs. DAT machines are widely used in both project and professional studios because of their widespread usage and convenient media.

DAT tapes are like tiny video cassettes that can hold up to two hours of audio at 16-bit, 44.1/48kHz resolution, although most professionals are wary of anything over 90 minutes in length. Recording is straightforward, as long as you ensure that the input level never hits the clip LED at the top of the meter. Because DAT uses a rotating-head system like that of a video recorder the actual tape speed is extremely slow, so it's usual to leave between 30 seconds and a minute of tape blank at the start of the tape just in case any dropouts occur near the start. Unlike analogue tape, however, DAT machines record a subcode derived from the sample clock, even when the audio input is silence, so you should record silence from the start of the tape rather than wind to the one minute mark and record from there. Similarly, for the time counter to work properly the subcode must be continuous, which means that, when you want to add more material to a tape onto which you've already recorded material, you should wind back to a point at which the previous subcode is recognised before you resume recording. Clearly this means allowing the recorder to run on for a little after each recording, in order to lay down a few extra seconds of subcode. Failure to maintain a contiguous subcode in this way will confuse the real-time counter – for example, it may start again from zero after a section of unrecorded tape.

MiniDisc

MiniDisc is a consumer audio format that uses an aggressive data compression system to reduce the amount of data needed to represent a given length of audio. Essentially, anything that the compression algorithm thinks is rendered inaudible through masking by other parts of the music is discarded. Because of this compression MiniDisc is not as accurate as DAT, but it's still good enough to use for demos or independent releases of pop music with a limited dynamic range. Indeed, most people can't distinguish it from CDs, although a discerning listener can usually spot the difference, especially on classical material. I would recommend mixing onto DAT if possible, but MiniDisc will suffice for all but the most demanding applications.

SCMS

SCMS (Serial Copy Management System) was introduced after the record companies pressured manufacturers into producing a device which could protect their works from piracy in the digital domain. SCMS is implemented by almost all consumer digital recording hardware, and works by inserting an invisible flag in the data stream. Depending on the status of this flag, the recording you make can be copied freely, copied for one generation (so that the copies can't be used to make further copies) or copying can be prohibited altogether. A source recording can be copied digitally but a flag is inserted in the new copy which will prevent any machine fitted with SCMS from making any further copies from it. Of course, you can make as many copies as you like from the original, and you can still copy in the analogue domain, so the system is actually more of a nuisance to bona fide studio users than it is a deterrent to pirates, as you usually end up with 'copy prohibited' flags on copies of your own material. Fortunately, most computer-based editing systems strip out the SCMS flag.

CD-R

Now that blank CD-Rs are cheaper than analogue cassettes, they have become very attractive for those wishing to archive audio data from sequencers as well as for storing final stereo mixes. Computer-based CD-R recorders are fairly easy to use if they are issued with decent software, and the discs are reasonably durable as long as they are handled carefully and stored in a dark, dust-free environment. You should avoid cutting corners by using cheap, unbranded discs, as you may end up losing valuable data, and try not to get dust and fingermarks on the discs before recording onto them, as this can cause problems when during the burning process.

Now that it's possible to record, mix and master material without it ever leaving your computer, it's possible to burn a CD directly without having to master your material to DAT or MiniDisc. Rewritable CD-Rs are also useful for recording audio data from your sequencer, but they'll normally only play back on a CD writer, not a computer CD-ROM drive or audio CD player. However, some of the new generation of consumer CD players will work with CD-R, and it's possible that future models will do this as standard.

chapter 3

the soundcard studio

In the past music studios were complex and costly affairs, comprising open-reel tape machines, synchronisers, huge mixers, MIDI sequencers, sound modules, keyboards, outboard effects and miles and miles of cabling, but the possibilities offered by the computer desktop studio means that it no longer has to be this way.

Computer soundcards have received a lot of bad press in the past, mainly because of the very cheap models that are supplied as standard with PCs, enabling their owners to play games. Fortunately, a number of serious manufacturers have turned their attentions to designing soundcards, and have produced models on which the audio converters do justice to 16- or 24-bit audio and, where provided, on-board synthesis capability is derived from either existing keyboard instruments or sound modules which cost three or four times as much. What's more, because PC soundcards are purely software-driven devices, there is often a surprising amount of useful support software bundled into the card, including sequencers, editor librarians, MIDI song files and mixer maps for the most commonly-used sequencers. As mentioned previously, choosing a card with multiple inputs and outputs is likely to cost more than a stereo in/stereo out card, but even multichannel cards start at a very reasonable price when you consider how much open-reel tape recorders used to cost.

As a very general rule, the soundcards that are also capable of synthesising and interfacing with MIDI have evolved from the games market, and usually offer stereo analogue ins and outs, with the better models also offering S/PDIF ins and outs. Multiple input and output systems are more often designed to provide audio-only support, so you may need to look elsewhere for synthesis and MIDI interfacing.

Because PCs have a number of expansion slots it's possible to use two or more soundcards in the same machine, although installing hardware isn't always the painless procedure it ought to be, particularly if the cards are of different types. In most cases it's probably best to choose a single card that provides the necessary features, or to use two cards of the same type to increase the amount of available I/O. The newer PCI cards used with Windows '95 are relatively easy to install, but you can still run into trouble if you've never delved into the nuts and bolts of computer operating systems before, so I make no excuses for once again advising you to buy a fully-installed and -configured system if at all possible.

Macintosh users

Both Macs and PCs now use PCI card slots, so both systems can use soundcards in much the same way, although, unlike PCs, all modern Macs come with basic 16-bit audio interfacing built in. Stereo inputs and outputs are accessed via mini jacks, which can be selected as the audio input and output devices via the Sound control panel of the Mac. If you have any other Sound-Manager-compatible audio hardware installed, this control panel will allow you to select between Mac internal hardware and the installed hardware. Although the sound quality produced by these internal converters isn't as good as that produced by a high-quality audio interface or a dedicated card, it's still good enough for serious demo work.

connections

While a cheap soundcard plugged into a pair of nasty little powered AV monitors isn't going to threaten the conventional studio, the more serious user can gain access to some pretty serious music power on a computer for very little additional expense. What's more, it's often possible to mix and process sounds in a far more comprehensive manner than you might imagine. For example, there may be several separate stereo outputs running from different soundcards and daughterboards that can be conventionally mixed with an external analogue or digital mixer. While there's usually an option to daisy-chain the audio ins and outs of various soundcards to enable you to mix everything into stereo, the quality of the sound drops off significantly if mixed in this way, and by keeping outputs separate it's possible to patch into an external mixer, which is far more flexible.

A digital studio doesn't have to be completely digital. In a simple setup a small analogue mixer is the most cost-effective model to use, because it provides high-quality sound, you can patch in outboard effects if necessary, and you don't have to worry about sample rates and synchronising if you're looking to add material from other digital sources, such as CD players, DAT machines and MiniDisc recorders. Keeping a few mixer inputs spare is always a good idea, as sooner or later you'll be tempted to add a hardware synth or a sampler to your system.

Monitoring can be carried out on a proper monitoring system or a hi-fi rather than on cheap, powered desktop speakers, and with the improved audio quality provided by an external mixer you can produce a very respectable mix, especially if you master to DAT or MiniDisc rather than analogue cassette. There are also other reasons why adding a mixer is often a good idea.

While PC soundcards often come with mic or line inputs that allow you to record your own .WAV audio files (the standard PC sound file), the signal path through these is usually pretty poor and they have no provision for connecting professional-quality studio mics.

A much better option is to use an external mixer or mic pre-amp to bring the output from a decent mic up to line level and then feed this into the soundcard's line input. Not only does this allow you to use a studio-quality mic but it will also improve the signal-to-noise ratio of your recording by amplifying the signal within the mixer, rather than within the soundcard.

Even if you're using a fairly basic general-purpose mixer you can use one channel as a mic pre-amp simply by turning the channel fader right down and using the channel insert send to feed your soundcard. The mic gain is set with the channel's gain trim facility, and the signal level is monitored with whatever facilities are provided with the soundcard. Figure 3.1 illustrates how a typical PC-based system might be connected.

Figure 3.1: A typical soundcard studio

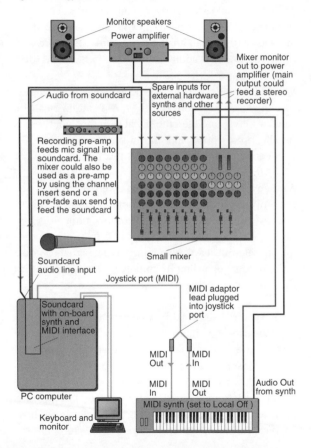

Monitor speakers

Power amplifier

Mixer monitor out to power amplifier (main output could feed a stereo recorder)

Audio from soundcard

Spare inputs for external hardware synths and other sources

Recording pre-amp feeds mic signal into soundcard. The mixer could also be used as a pre-amp by using the channel insert send or a pre-fade aux send to feed the soundcard

Small mixer

Soundcard audio line input

Joystick port (MIDI)

MIDI adaptor lead plugged into joystick port

Soundcard with on-board synth and MIDI interface

MIDI Out

MIDI In

MIDI In

MIDI Out

Audio Out from synth

PC computer

Keyboard and monitor

MIDI synth (set to Local Off)

If your mixer has no insert points, you can instead use the pre-fade aux send on the mic channel to send the mic signal to the correspondingly-numbered aux send output and then use this to feed the soundcard input. For example, you could feed your mic into channel one and then route this to the aux one output by turning up the aux one send on only channel one. The level fader on channel one would be off, and the level would then be sent to the soundcard controlled by the aux one master output level knob.

Outboard effects may be connected to the mixer in the conventional way via post-fade aux sends and effects return channels. If you're not familiar with this aspect of mixers, the book *basic MIXERS* – also in this series – investigates them in some depth. Alternatively, you could consult your mixer's manual.

recording pre-amps

A number of companies produce recording pre-amps that combine a high-quality mic/line/instrument pre-amp with a compressor and an equaliser. These devices plug directly into the line input of a soundcard and enable you to record with a high-quality studio mic. Electric guitars and basses may be plugged into the high-impedance instrument input, while line-level sources, such as keyboards, may be recorded via the line input. The compressor produces a more even sound, and compression is invariably used on vocals in commercial recordings. With a high-quality equaliser you can adjust the tone of the sound before it is recorded, and if you prefer to record one track at a time then the best way of ensuring the optimum sound quality is to use a recording pre-amp, as the mic section on a pre-amp is generally better than those found on low- to mid-priced mixers.

and there's MIDI

A basic PC MIDI system will generally use the MIDI interface provided by the soundcard, and the standard way of working in this case is to use a MIDI adaptor cable, which plugs into the card's joystick port.

Simple one in/one out MIDI interfaces are limited in that you can only drive 16 external MIDI channels from them. With today's synth modules this usually means a single multitimbral instrument, but you should remember that all internal soundcards (except the daughterboard) use virtual MIDI ports in order to avoid tying up the external MIDI port. This is obviously good news if you're on a strict budget, as you can then use the sounds present on your internal soundcard at the same time as one multitimbral external MIDI module and still only need one MIDI port.

If you need more ports in order to handle additional external synths then you can buy multiport MIDI interfaces, as either cards or external hardware boxes, which offer eight or more sets of MIDI outputs. These interfaces should not be confused with simple multi-output Thru boxes, however, from which each MIDI Out carries the same information – a multiport interface's outputs are quite independent, and are usually identified by numbers or by letters. For example, port A would carry MIDI channels 1-16A while port B would carry channels 1-16B, and so on. An eight-output multiport interface provides 128 MIDI channels, all of which can be addressed separately, and this should be sufficient for all but the most equipment-intensive arrangements. It's important to check that the interface you are considering is designed to work with the audio software which you intend to use.

A 'dumb' MIDI master keyboard can be simply connected to the computer's MIDI In, while a MIDI synth keyboard would need to be set to Local Off so that the synth section could be driven from the MIDI Out port of the computer. Figure 3.1 shows the configuration of this latter option.

evolution

The PC- or Mac-based MIDI/audio studio has the advantages of being relatively inexpensive, compact and (once set up) convenient. With the addition of a mixer, a monitoring system and possibly some outboard signal processing you should have the basis of a serious desktop music recording system at your fingertips, and as soundcards continue to become more powerful and better specified it's possible to upgrade a system a piece at a time without having to sell up and start from scratch. However, it's wise to buy the fastest computer you can afford because, as new software versions become available, they always include new features that make more demands on your processor. By choosing your soundcard or audio interface carefully, and incorporating a small mixer along with a modest amount of external signal processing, it's possible to build a serious desktop studio for less money than stereo samplers used to cost.

software synthesis

Software-based synthesis (ie that which uses the computer's own processing power to create sounds, rather than hardware) is becoming more practical now that high-powered computers are relatively cheap. Obviously, these packages use up some of the computer's processing power and memory, and this can be anything from just a few percent up to nearly the entire processing power of the system, depending on the software's sophistication and how well written it is.

latency and monitoring

Latency is one aspect of working with the soundcard studio around which manufacturers tend to skirt, and often users don't understand its full implications until they've already parted with their money. Latency is that infuriating delay which occurs between the sound being fed into a computer-based recording system and re-emerging from the audio outs. Latency arises when audio is routed via the host processor (which is necessary if you wish to monitor the sound while software plug-in effects are running), and because of the way in which the computer operating system handles data this round trip can take a noticeable amount of time. You can also hear the effects of latency when you hit the Start button to play back a sequence, as there is often a short delay before playback actually begins.

On a well-designed system this latency may only be a few milliseconds, in which case few people will even notice it's there; but other combinations of hardware and software can throw up delays of more than half a second. As a rule, latency is only a serious problem when overdubbing, when whatever you're trying to overdub comes back with delay added. This can throw out your timing if the delay is too great.

There are both hardware and software approaches to minimising latency, notably Steinberg's ASIO II drivers (software) and soundcards with integral DSP effects and thru monitoring (hardware). Thru monitoring simply means that, when overdubbing, the audio passes straight through the soundcard and onto the monitor outputs without going through the computer's CPU. But if you already have a system and latency is giving you trouble, what can be done?

input monitoring

The answer is to use a mixer to set up the monitoring. Unless you have an extremely simple system, and you rely on the same soundcard to provide synth sounds and audio recording, you'll probably already use a mixer to combine the output from your soundcard with the outputs from your external synths, samplers and drum machines. Furthermore, unless you're going to trust all of your audio processing to VST plug-ins or similar computer-powered virtual devices, you'll need a recording pre-amp with an integral compressor, which will even out vocal levels during the recording stage.

Assuming that you're in possession of this equipment, you can now set up a simple system in which the output from your recording pre-amp is split to feed both the mixer and the soundcard input. At it's simplest this could be done with a Y-lead (it's always alright to split signals this way but not to mix them), but you'll find that many recording pre-amps already have two outputs, often one on a jack and the other on an XLR. If this is the case, you can feed the jack output to the soundcard and then make up a balanced-XLR-to-balanced-quarter-inch jack lead to feed the mixer's line input. You might be able to get away with using an XLR lead plugged directly into the mixer mic input, but only if your mixer has a pad switch and plenty of attenuation range on the input gain trim.

If you don't have a recording pre-amp you may instead be able to use one of your mixing channels, as long as it has a direct output (or insert send) to feed to the soundcard input. This will allow you to monitor your overdub directly through the mixer when recording, but you'll need to mute the output from the track being recorded within your software or you'll hear both the direct monitor signal and the delayed signal. Some packages have a thru monitoring on/off switch, while with others you simply have to use the software's virtual mixing facilities to turn down or mute the output from the track being recorded.

After you've recorded your material you'll need to unmute the track output before you can hear it (if you killed the delayed monitor signal by muting it, that is), and you may also want to mute the mixer channel on which you monitored your recording pre-amp or your live mic will still be feeding the mix. However, this system is limited in that, because you're bypassing the computer when monitoring overdubs, you won't be able to hear the effects of any VST plug-ins until after the track has been recorded. If you need to apply reverb to help the singer provide accurate vocals, you can still hook up a regular hardware effects unit to your mixer and add as much monitor reverb or echo as you like – it won't be recorded. The complete setup is shown in Figure 3.2.

punching in

If you're executing a punch in to patch up a mistake in your recording, using thru monitoring means that you won't be able to hear the original track, as it will be

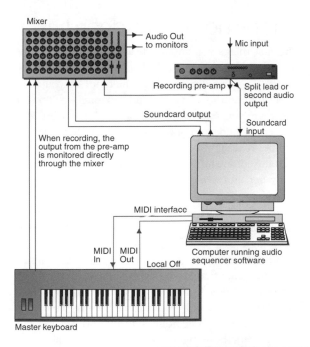

Figure 3.2: Thru monitoring via a mixer

turned down or muted. A practical solution to this problem is to record the punch-in part on a new track and then paste it into the original track once you've got it right. It's easier to edit vocals if you can punch in and out between words.

choosing a soundcard

The first things you should decide is whether or not you need a stereo or multichannel card. How many tracks do you need to record at one time? Do you need to get them out of the computer separately, or do you plan on mixing internally? Applications like Cubase VST and Logic Audio are powerful in that they allow a number of audio tracks to be recorded separately and then mixed down. The mixing is carried out inside the computer, and so is possible with just a stereo output.

Many soundcards now offer better than 16-bit resolution, but both 20- and 24-bit recordings take 50% more hard disk space than 16 bit. 18-, 20- or 24-bit converters are used because they provide more dynamic range than 16-bit converters, but unless the rest of your studio equipment is of superb quality these extra bits will probably record only the hiss from your mic pre-amps or traffic noise. If the card you're looking to buy offers these higher bit depths then by all means try them to check if you can hear a difference, but if you're recording regular pop music you'll save a lot of hard drive space by switching to 16-bit operation.

If you need to send audio from your computer to a digital stereo recorder, such as a DAT or MiniDisc machine, you'll need a card with a digital output, and it's best to get a card with both digital ins and outs to provide you with more flexibility. The most common consumer digital interface is S/PDIF (Sony/Philips Digital InterFace), and there are two types available: the more common is co-axial (which uses phono sockets), but there is also a version, known as Toslink, which uses fibre-optic cables. I mention this because you need to ensure that the S/PDIF connector on your soundcard matches that on your recorder. There are adaptors available which convert between the two, but this is just needless expense.

Professional audio equipment uses AES/EBU, a balanced system which uses XLR connectors, although these aren't used on budget soundcards. S/PDIF will prove to be adequate in most instances.

After deciding exactly how many input and output channels you're going to need, you should look at the other features you may need, such as on-board synths, MIDI interfaces, hardware mixing and effects. Furthermore, you should also find out whether daughterboards can be added later, thus increasing the synthesis capabilities of the card. If you choose a card that can handle sampling, make sure that there is provision for adding more sample RAM (unless the card is designed to use the computer's own system RAM).

soundcard drivers

You'll need a piece of software called a driver to make a soundcard work with your audio software. Cards are useless without the right drivers, and the quality of the driver can dramatically affect the amount of latency you have to endure. The driver is usually part of the package that comes with the card, but if the card happens to be made by the same company that makes your audio software you might find that the audio software has the necessary driver already built in. It's also quite common for driver software to be updated in order to improve its performance or to iron out any bugs, and the best way to obtain an up-to-date driver is to make frequent visits to the card vendor's web site, where the most current downloads are often available. The most popular audio software is compatible with Steinberg's ASIO (Audio-Specific Input Output) driver standard, so if you want to use this you should make sure that ASIO drivers are available for your card. And if you find all of this stuff about drivers a little heavy, then that's just one more reason to buy a complete, working system.

BeOS

Most PCs run on Microsoft's Windows software, but this isn't ideal for music programs because it's designed as a broad platform to support a number of different types of software, from word processing and Internet browsers to graphics and spreadsheets. Be Corporation have developed an alternative operating system that runs on suitably-specified PCs and on pre-G3 PowerPC Macintoshes. This operating system is known as BeOS (Be Operating System), and is specifically designed to handle multimedia work effectively and with very low audio latency. The catch is that software must be designed to run on BeOS – you can't just load up a Windows program. Fortunately, several major audio software manufacturers are already developing versions of their programs for use with the BeOS. At a recent demonstration I tried a software synthesis package on both BeOS and Windows '98, and while the Windows version had around half a second of latency, rendering it unplayable, the BeOS synth responded so quickly that it was just like playing a hardware instrument. A low latency is obviously very important with software instruments, because any appreciable delay will prevent you from playing in time. The range of music software that will run on BeOS is for the moment fairly limited, but from what I've seen so far the BeOS system could make the PC a much better platform for audio than it is currently with Microsoft's Windows software.

no games!

The secret of having a smooth-running PC-based studio is to use it for only music. If you picked a PC for the kids to play games, or to surf the Internet, you could be heading for trouble. Games often take over certain resources and operate in unorthodox ways to get the maximum performance out of the game, and you may find that they mess up the way in which your audio software runs. If you need to use a PC for two distinct areas of work, it may be best to get a dual boot drive system with a separate copy of Windows installed on each drive and switch between them, using one drive exclusively for music and the other for all of your non-music applications.

On the Mac OS it's possible to select your start-up drive. However, even a dual boot system may not be necessary, as you can use the Extensions Manager control panel to create a customised set of extensions specifically designed for music use, with all unnecessary extensions switched off. In this way you don't need two versions of the Mac OS on different drives – you can simply start up with the appropriate set of extensions. Again, if you're new to this aspect of computing, ask a computer specialist (or a friend who has already gone through this) to help you out.

music software

No matter which computer platform you finally choose, the ultimate functionality of your system will be determined by the software you buy to run on it. Music software tends to fall into a number of main categories: MIDI sequencers, MIDI-plus-audio sequencers, multitrack recorders (which are much like sequencers but with no MIDI capabilities), stereo editors, effects and processor plug-ins, and virtual synths. There are also programs that fall between the serious sequencer and hobbyist categories, most of which function by using and ·processing existing musical loops and sound samples.

the sequencer

A modern MIDI sequencer will provide a bare minimum of 16 MIDI tracks (often many more), and most now include some level of audio support. With a MIDI sequencer, numerous separate musical parts can be recorded at different times, either through the parts being played one at a time on a MIDI keyboard, through note and timing data being entered manually, or through a combination of 'live' playing and editing. Once recorded, these parts may be played back via any MIDI-compatible synthesiser or collection of synths.

You'll also need a synthesiser (either a keyboard instrument or a MIDI module), unless you have a soundcard with one already built in, and the number of different musical parts that can be played back simultaneously depends on the number and type of the synthesisers that are at your disposal. Fortunately, most modern synthesisers and PC soundcards are capable of playing back a minimum of 16 different sounds at once, each controlled by a different MIDI channel. This ability is known as multitimbrality.

the MIDI composer

Although the MIDI musician uses a lot of electronics, the process of composing with MIDI isn't that different from the traditional approach to composing. Like orchestral composition the work usually starts at the keyboard, but in this case the keyboard is a MIDI instrument connected to a MIDI sequencer, rather than a piano. Instead of writing down a score the composer records sections of the music into the sequencer against an electronic metronome set to the desired tempo, and instead of scanning a score to verify what's been done the composer simply plays back the recording on a suitable synthesiser in order to hear exactly what's been recorded. A multitimbral synthesiser can play several musical parts at once, and when used in conjunction with a sequencer each 'part' of the multitimbral synth can be used to play back one musical part. For example, you might have two sequencer tracks dedicated to strings, one to horns, one to percussion and one to woodwind.

MIDI and sequencing

It's often convenient to visualise a sequencer as being analogous to a multitrack tape recorder, but it's vitally important to remember that, with MIDI, what is being recorded is not the sound itself but the electronic equivalent of a musical score. Just as a musical score is a series of instructions to the musicians, a MIDI sequence contains a series of instructions which tell your synths what to play and when to play it.

audio sequencers

The audio tracks within a MIDI-plus-audio sequencer record digitised audio directly onto your computer's hard drive. These tracks may be edited in much the same way as MIDI tracks, so the ability to manipulate

MIDI and audio together within the same environment is very attractive if you enjoy experimenting with different arrangements. Unlike tape recording, MIDI tracks can be divided into sections, and these sections can then be moved to different locations in a song. Furthermore, the same sections may be used two or more times without re-recording the part, so if you want to you can use the same backing vocals on every chorus. Similarly, a short section of drums can be looped and repeated to provide a continuous drum track.

sequencer setup

In a typical setup, a master MIDI controller (usually a keyboard, but not always) is connected to a sequencer with a MIDI cable, and when the sequencer is set to record, any notes played by the keyboard are recorded as MIDI data into whichever sequencer track has been selected for recording. A simple system might have 16 MIDI tracks set up so that each is on a different MIDI channel, and if the MIDI output of the sequencer is fed to a 16-part multitimbral module all 16 tracks can then be played back at once. If you only have an eight-part multitimbral module, however, only eight different sounds can be played back at once, just as a real-life eight-piece ensemble can only play a maximum of eight different lines of music at the same time. (Figure 3.1 in chapter three shows how a typical computer-based sequencing system connects to an external keyboard synth.) If you have a keyboard that includes a synth, as shown here, simply select Local Off and connect it up like any other synth module. Local Off isolates the synth's keyboard from its sound-generating circuitry so that, in effect, it behaves as if it were a separate dumb keyboard and MIDI synth module. This is necessary in preventing MIDI information from being fed around the system in a continuous loop, which usually causes trouble with stuck or repeating notes.

metronomes

Although a sequencer can be treated as nothing more than a multitrack MIDI recorder, its real power lies in the way in which it can modify or edit recorded data. When a recording is made, the sequencer is set to the tempo of the desired recording and a metronome click is laid down so that the musical performance can be synchronised with the internal tempo of the sequencer. In this way the MIDI data is arranged in musically meaningful bars, which makes editing note timing or copying and moving whole sections a very easy and precise procedure.

With music incorporating tempo changes it's possible to enter a new tempo at any bar or beat location, although some budget sequencers may impose a limit on the number of tempo changes which can be placed in each song. More sophisticated sequencers may even have a graphic Tempo Editing mode, in which smooth increases or decreases in tempo can be created by drawing slopes. If you don't want to be tied to a tempo at all, you can simply turn off the metronome click and play normally.

tracks and channels

At this point in the proceedings it's very easy to mix up MIDI channels and sequencer tracks, but they're very different. A sequencer track is simply somewhere to record one layer of your composition, but the MIDI information in that track can be on any MIDI channel you want. A track can even contain MIDI data relating to two or more MIDI channels, although mostly a single track records data on a single channel to avoid any confusion.

It's also possible to have several different tracks recording MIDI data set to the same channel. For example, if you're recording a complicated drum part you might want to lay the bass and snare drum onto one track, the cymbals and hi-hats onto another and any tom fills onto a third. All of the drum sounds may be on the same MIDI channel, but because they're on different tracks they're effectively recorded as different layers. Not only does this make the

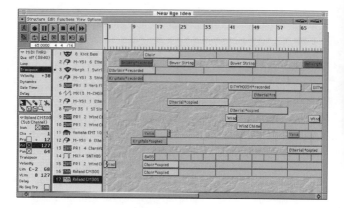

Figure 4.1: Sequencer Arrange page

parts easier to play but it also makes it less confusing
when editing in any changes. Figure 4.1 shows the
Arrange page of a popular computer-based sequencing
package, depicting the layout of the tracks and the way in
which recorded sequences are represented.

cut, copy and paste

The remaining capabilities of a MIDI sequencer bear
more resemblance to a word processor than anything
else. Like a word processor, you can delete or replace
wrong characters (in this case musical notes), and if you

want to use the same phrase more than once you can copy it and paste copies of it into new locations rather than having to play the same material several times.

MIDI information comprises not just note information but also controller data from modulation wheels, pitch-bend wheels, expression pedals and so forth. Unless you deliberately filter out certain types of MIDI data (and some sequencers have the facility to do this), you'll find that your sequencer captures note on, note off, velocity, pitch, modulation and aftertouch data, along with other controller information and MIDI Program Changes and Bank Change messages. When recording a part that needs the addition of a lot of complicated pitch bending or vibrato, a useful trick is to record the part straight onto one track and then record the vibrato and pitch-bend wheel data on another track set to the same MIDI channel. As you record the controller data track you'll hear it affecting the performance on the original track.

A sequencer track must also be informed of the synthesiser sound which it is expected to control, so in addition to the MIDI channel number (which tells the sequencer which instrument or which part of a multitimbral instrument it is controlling), it's also necessary to enter the program number of the patch you want to hear, and if the synthesiser supports MIDI Bank

Change messages you'ill also need to tell it in which bank the sound is located. For this reason it helps to photocopy the relevant patch lists from your synthesiser manuals and pin them to the wall next to your sequencer. If you're not very experienced with MIDI, the *basic MIDI* book in this series covers this area in greater detail.

playback

When a MIDI sequence is played back, the sequencer transmits the MIDI information to the receiving synth in exactly the same order and with exactly the same timing as it was originally played, although you can change the tempo after recording without affecting the pitch (unlike a tape recorder, which uses analogue sound rather than MIDI data). The level of each part in your composition can also be controlled with MIDI, usually by changing the value of MIDI controller seven (master volume). Most sequencers provide an easy way of doing this.

editing

On the editing pages of a typical sequencer it's possible to change the value, start time, length and velocity of any of the notes you've played, or you can build up compositions by entering the notes manually, placing new notes onto the quantise grid in non-real time, in much the same manner as writing out a manuscript. If you're working with a package that has a scoring facility, it's also possible to enter notes directly onto the score, almost as though you were writing notes on manuscript paper. The entry of note information in non-real time is sometimes known as step-time entry.

quantising

An important feature common to both hardware and software sequencers is the ability to quantise data after it has been recorded. This is useful for those users who don't have a perfect sense of timing. Essentially, when you choose to quantise something, the timing of your piece is changed so that every note you've recorded is pushed to the nearest exact subdivision of a bar. For example, if you're working in 4/4 time and you select 16 as your quantise value, every note moves to the nearest point on an invisible grid dividing the bar into 16 equal time slots.

The quantise function must be used carefully, however, as it can strip all of the 'feel' from some types of music; however, if you're working with dance music, with which precise timing is essential, the quantise function is indispensable. Remember that the quantise function will only produce meaningful results if your original recording was made in time with the sequencer's metronome click.

MIDI drums

Most soundcards and synths have built-in drum sounds, and traditionally these are often assigned to MIDI channel ten. Using drums is exactly the same as using any other keyboard sound, except that, instead of having the same sound playing at different pitches across the keyboard, each key will play back a different drum sound.

types of sequencer

All MIDI sequencers use computer technology, but you can choose between buying a sequencer system that runs on an existing computer (such as an Atari ST, Apple Macintosh, IBM PC or Commodore Amiga) or opting for a piece of dedicated hardware, on which everything you need is built into one box. These two groups work in a similar manner, and tend to vary only in the way in which the recorded information is displayed and how easily it can be edited. Hardware sequencers are also built into workstation-type keyboard synthesisers, and some hardware sequencers also have built-in synth modules.

Hardware sequencers offer relatively accomplished players the benefits of simplicity and convenience, but because they can't display as much information as a full-size computer screen, and because there's no mouse, editing is generally less comprehensive and more time consuming than it is on a computer-based system. However, recording usually involves little more than selecting a track, hitting Record and playing the material. Another benefit of hardware computers is that they are more practical in live performance situations – they are more compact and more rugged than a computer and monitor, and there's also not as much to plug in.

MIDI data storage

It's one thing to record a MIDI sequence, but what do you do with it once it's finished? There's no manuscript paper on which to store your work; song data is instead stored as a MIDI song file on a floppy disk or hard drive. Computer-based sequencers lose their stored information when they are switched off, so it's vital to save your work to disk at regular intervals. It's also an unfortunate fact that computers crash when you least expect it, so it pays to save your work every few minutes.

computer complexity

Computer-based sequencers are capable of considerably more sophistication than most hardware models, which means that they often have a steeper learning curve. You must always familiarise yourself with the general operation of the computer before trying to tackle a sequencer package, although in my opinion this is more than compensated by the amount of visual control available, especially when it comes to creating new song arrangements or editing recorded material.

the MIDI interface

On a hardware sequencer you simply plug your master keyboard into the MIDI In socket, plug a synthesiser into the MIDI Out socket and you're ready to go. Computers, on the other hand, don't usually have MIDI sockets – the obvious exception being the popular but now-ageing Atari ST. This means that, unless you're using one of these, you'll need to buy an external MIDI interface, one of the synth modules that comes with a built-in MIDI interface, or a soundcard that has MIDI In and Out ports.

MIDI interfaces for Macintoshes plug into the modem or printer ports on the back of the computer, while PC users need either a soundcard fitted into their computers or an external plug-in interface. Most PC multimedia cards include a MIDI interface facility, although it may be necessary to buy a special adaptor cable to make use of it.

basic digital recording

```
┌─────────────────────────────────────────────────────────┐
│              New Age Id...:Etherial*copied               │
│ ▪ Edit Functions View                                    │
│       POSITION        STATUE   CHA  NUM  VAL  LENGTH/INFO │
│      --------- Start of List ---------                   │
│       21  1  1   1    NOTE  1   B1   25   3  3  1  220    │
│       21  1  1   1    NOTE  1   E2   32   3  3  1  216    │
│       21  1  1   1    NOTE  1   G#2  12   3  3  1   80    │
│       21  1  1   1    NOTE  1   C#3  17   3  3  1  168    │
│       21  1  1   1    NOTE  1   D#3  18   3  3  1   60    │
│       25  1  1   1    NOTE  1   G#1 103   3  3  3  232    │
│       25  1  1   1    NOTE  1   E2  103   3  3  3  232    │
│       25  1  1   1    NOTE  1   G#2 103   3  3  3  232    │
│       25  1  1   1    NOTE  1   D#3 103   3  3  3  232    │
│       25  1  1   1    NOTE  1   G#3 103   3  3  3  232    │
│       29  1  1   1    NOTE  1   F#1  97   3  3  3   52    │
│       29  1  1   1    NOTE  1   D#2  97   3  3  3   52    │
│       29  1  1   1    NOTE  1   C#3  97   3  3  3   52    │
│       33  1  1   1    NOTE  1   G#1  97   3  3  3   52    │
│       33  1  1   1    NOTE  1   C#2  97   3  3  3   52    │
│       33  1  1   1    NOTE  1   A#2  97   3  3  3   52    │
│       37  1  1   1    NOTE  1   B1   97   3  3  3   52    │
│       37  1  1   1    NOTE  1   E2   97   3  3  3   52    │
│       37  1  1   1    NOTE  1   G#2  97   3  3  3   52    │
│       37  1  1   1    NOTE  1   C#3  97   3  3  3   52    │
│       37  1  1   1    NOTE  1   B3   97   3  3  3   52    │
│      --------- End of List ---------                     │
└─────────────────────────────────────────────────────────┘
```

Figure 4.2: Sequencer Edit pages

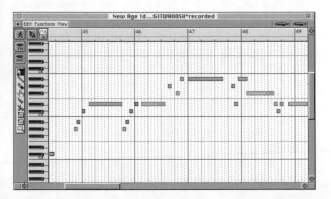

100

Figure 4.2: Sequencer Edit pages

the user interface

Most of the market-leading software sequencing
packages have adopted the style of interface which
was pioneered by Steinberg in their Cubase software.
The success of this interface is based around the fact
that it uses a digital analogy of multitrack tape. The
sequencer tracks are depicted on the computer
screen as individual vertically-stacked strips, with
musical bars running sequentially from left to right.
Once a section of a track has been recorded it is
shown as a brick running from the start location to
the end location. This sequence may then be dragged
with the mouse to a new position in the same track,
or it may even be moved to a completely different
track so that it plays back with a different sound.

Sequence blocks may also be copied, split into shorter sections or deleted as required.

Most software sequencers comprise a main page, on which to handle basic recording and arranging, along with a number of other pages addressing various aspects of editing and, where applicable, scoring. The Record and Playback controls are invariably designed to look something like a tape recorder's transport control buttons, and the Edit pages usually allow you to examine and change the recorded data as a list of MIDI events either graphically, as a display resembling the roll of a player piano, or as a conventional music score. Most sequencers also have graphic editing capabilities for editing controller information. Figure 4.2 shows some of the Edit pages from a popular software sequencer.

Some software sequencing packages also include sophisticated score-writing facilities, which enable you to print out sheet music of your compositions, although to achieve this you'll need a printer which is compatible both with your computer and the software package. Also, because the computer doesn't always interpret what is played in the same way that a trained score writer would, some musical literacy is also useful.

extra MIDI ports

Basic MIDI interfaces provide single MIDI output sockets, which means that a maximum of 16 MIDI channels are available to the user. However, you may wish to use two or more multitimbral synthesisers to create a composition with more than 16 parts, or – as is more often the case – you may wish to change between a number of synthesiser modules without having to reconnect MIDI leads. This can be achieved by using a MIDI interface with multiple output ports.

It's impossible to have than 16 MIDI channels, but if a multi-port MIDI interface is used in conjunction with compatible sequencing software it's possible to have several different sets of 16 MIDI channels. The ports may be designated by number or letter within the sequencer, so that there are 16 channels on port A, another 16 on port B and a further 16 on port C. If a different 16-part multitimbral synth module is connected to each of these ports then this means that 48 different sound sources are available, each of which can be addressed individually by specifying a MIDI channel and a port letter (A, B or C). Figure 4.3 shows how such a multiport system might be configured. It's important to realise, however, that your multiport interface must be supported by the sequencing software you choose, and lists of suitable interfaces are usually

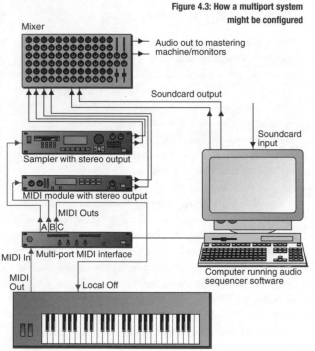

Figure 4.3: How a multiport system might be configured

Mixer

Audio out to mastering machine/monitors

Soundcard output

Soundcard input

Sampler with stereo output

MIDI module with stereo output

MIDI Outs

A B C

Multi-port MIDI interface

MIDI In

MIDI Out

Local Off

Computer running audio sequencer software

Master keyboard

displayed in sequencer manuals, but consult your dealer if you're in any doubt at all. Hardware-based sequencers tend to have only one or two output ports, and with no means for future expansion this constitutes one of their greatest limitations in a complex MIDI setup.

common problems

A basic MIDI sequencing setup will start at the keyboard – it's here that the MIDI information originates before it's recorded. The master keyboard is connected via its MIDI Out to the MIDI In of a MIDI interface or directly to the MIDI In of a hardware sequencer or Atari ST. If your keyboard includes a synth section (if it makes sounds, in other words) then switch it to Local Off and patch a MIDI cable from the sequencer's MIDI Out to the keyboard's MIDI In. If you have other MIDI modules connected to the system, these can be daisy-chained in any order by feeding the MIDI Thru of one piece of equipment to the MIDI In of the next. Alternatively, a Thru box can be used.

If your master keyboard doesn't have a Local Off facility, consult your sequencer manual to see if you can disable the MIDI Thru on the channel to which your master keyboard is set. Most sequencers provide for this.

Up to three modules can normally be chained in this Out-to-Thru setup without problems, but longer chains can cause notes to be stuck or missed (due to the MIDI signal becoming corrupted), in which case you should use a multiple-output MIDI Thru box on the output of your sequencer and then feed each module (or a short chain of two or three modules) from separate outputs on the Thru box.

MIDI timing

MIDI has a measurable timing resolution because the computer's internal timing routine is based on an electronic clock. However, MIDI is still much more accurate than a human performer and is capable of resolving a 4/4 bar of music into at least 960 time divisions. Some software extends this to an even finer degree of resolution, but there are still situations that can cause timing problems.

MIDI is a serial data protocol, which means that all data moves in single file. Because the data speed is reasonably high this isn't usually a problem, but if too much data is sent at once – for example, if all 16 channels try to play a large musical chord at exactly the same time – this results in a musical traffic jam, causing the notes to be spread out slightly. Using a lot of other MIDI control data can also slow things up, but the better sequencing software packages reduce this problem by giving priority to note timing.

In most musical compositions MIDI timing shouldn't be an issue, but if problems do arise one tip is to put the most time-sensitive parts, such as drums, onto the lowest-numbered MIDI channels and less critical parts, such as slow-attack strings, onto higher-numbered tracks, in which case the lower channel numbers will be dealt with first. Also, if you need to have a lot of parts playing at once, a modern multiport MIDI interface with intelligent buffering, such as EMagic's AMT series, will tighten up the timing noticeably.

All but the most basic sequencers provide some facility for automating features such as MIDI level and pan, so that sounds can be programmed to change in level or move from one side to another automatically every time the track is played back. This automation works by providing easy access to MIDI controller information, often in the form of graphic displays which can be moved to create fades, level changes and so on.

sequencers with audio

Using a sequencer with audio isn't very different from using the MIDI-only version and the quality of the recording is limited only by the type of audio soundcard you have and the quality of the signal fed into it. On all of the major sequencers, the audio tracks can be mixed down into stereo within the sequencer, with full control over channel level and pan at the very least.

When a track is recorded it's actually saved as a file on the hard drive, but it also shows up on the sequencer Arrange page. Here the part can be dragged to new time locations or even dragged onto a different audio track. It's normally possible to divide the audio parts into smaller sections and move these parts around independently, although it's also important to note that none of these functions actually change the audio file that has been recorded onto the hard drive.

Depending on the sophistication of the audio package, you may also be able to edit the audio down to the waveform level, though be warned that most edits at this level are destructive (ie they affect the original file). Those edits routinely available include the ability to change audio levels, reverse files (so that they play backwards), create fade-ins and -outs and replace unwanted regions with silence. Further functionality may also be provided, depending on the sophistication of the software package; for example, there may be functions which can independently change the pitch or duration of a file.

Once the audio material has been recorded and moved into place, the mixing side of the program will invariably allow the tracks to be balanced and panned. Most serious sequencers also provide MIDI-controlled audio automation so that operations such as the movement of level and pan control can be recorded and stored. This will allow you to fine tune your mix until everything is perfect, and then, every time it's played back, it will have the right levels and the right moves.

The number of tracks that can be played back at any time will depend both on the speed of your hard drive and on the power of the computer. Unlike tape machines, on a sequencer it's usually possible to record as many tracks as is desirable, as long as you don't try to play back more than the system will allow at any one time. You could record a dozen takes of a solo and then choose the best one from this group, for example, and as long as you only play one version at a time it only counts as one track. All you need do is mute the tracks you're not using. The ability to store alternative takes is often known as having virtual tracks.

The mixing capabilities of a MIDI-plus-audio sequencer will offer level and pan control at the very least, but they will also often offer EQ. Unless you have specialised hardware, such as a card system with its own DSP (Digital Signal Processing) facilities, EQ is implemented with the host CPU's (Central Processing Unit's) own processing power. In practice this may mean that, unless you have a very powerful computer, the amount of EQ you can use is limited. Similarly, there may also be computer-driven effects, such as reverb or delay, which also obtain their power from the computer. Because not all manufacturers of sequencers specialise in audio processing, more advanced processing functions are usually available in the form of plug-ins.

software plug-ins

Once the sole domain of specialised hardware, many of the traditional recording and signal-processing tasks are now available in software form, either running on the native processing power of Macs and PCs or on DSP cards optimised for audio applications. For the more sophisticated user, who may need to run a number of powerful processing and mixing applications at the same time, a typical desktop computer may have insufficient processing power, in which case the use of a DSP-based audio interface system is recommended. However, modern computers should be able to run several plug-ins and many channels of EQ without running out of steam.

third-party plug-ins

Plug-in effects and processing software is available from a number of third-party suppliers, which means that the functionality of the host software may be extended in various ways. Different versions may be required depending on whether the host system runs on a Mac or PC, however, and on whether the effects are to run on the native processor or on a DSP system. DSP chips are not generally compatible with those of a different design, and new generations of DSP are appearing all the time, so it's important to make sure that you buy the correct version of plug-in for your system. For example, Digidesign's DSP-based ProTools hardware will run their own TDM plug-in format but won't run Steinberg's VST.

At the time of writing, the most common standard for real-time plug-ins using the computer's native processing power is VST (Virtual Studio Technology). VST was created by Steinberg, the manufacturers of Cubase, but was then opened up to all of the major music software companies in order to promote compatibility. VST plug-ins are available for both Mac and PC platforms, and are supported by a large number of third-party software writers. The standard VST II plug-in expands on the original concept by allowing plug-ins to read MIDI information from the host sequencer. For example, a pitch-shifting plug-in may be able to read MIDI notes directly from a sequencer track, while a delay or modulation plug-in may be able to link its activities to the track's tempo. Indeed, because a VST II plug-in can read MIDI note data it's possible to build a VST plug-in synth – and yes, Steinberg have done that too!

native plug-ins

Native plug-ins rely entirely on the host computer's processor and memory for their operation, and the amount of plug-ins that can be run at the same time will depend on the size of the processor. Some plug-ins require more processing power than others, and a good reverb package can use up a significant proportion of your processing resources. Sophisticated de-noising and de-clicking software is also processor intensive.

One way around the need for a powerful processor is to use a non-real-time plug-in such as AudioSuite or Premier. These generally allow the user to audition a short loop of audio held in RAM while adjusting the various parameters, after which the entire audio file or section of file is processed off line (which is, in effect, a destructive edit). Depending on the type of software package used with the plug-in, it will be deployed in different ways – real-time effects may be patched in via virtual channel or buss insert points, or aux sends and returns, although, on stereo editing packages which have no mixing facility, the plug-ins may be inserted in line with the audio output.

multiple plug-ins

One of the advantages of using plug-in effects and processors is that there's no wiring to worry about –

they don't take up any space in your studio and don't require a patchbay to be connected into the system. Furthermore, all settings are saved along with song data, so it's not necessary to remember which effects were used or how much of each was added to each channel.

Some DSP-based systems (such as Digidesign's widely-supported TDM platform) allow a single plug-in to provide multiple occurrences of the same processor, each with different settings. For example, you may be able to load in a compressor plug-in and then use six of those compressors in different channels of the virtual mixer, all optimised for different programme material. The practical limit on how many occurrences of a plug-in may be used at the same time is the amount of DSP processing power and RAM available, although some plug-in manufacturers may also build a limit into their software. More sophisticated systems allow additional DSP cards to be installed when more processing capability is needed.

types of plug-in

Virtually any effect or processor that can exist in hardware form can be built into a plug-in – indeed, there are direct software equivalents of famous-name compressors, equalisers, gates and reverbs, as well as any number of general-purpose EQs, delays and so on. Although digital emulations of specific analogue processors are not always entirely accurate, there are several digital processes that can be carried out more effectively in a software format, not least because of the more sophisticated displaying and interfacing possibilities accorded by the computer.

In addition to the more obvious processes, plug-ins can also handle de-noising, de-clicking and other high-level tasks, such as azimuth correction on analogue tape masters made on improperly aligned machines. Plug-ins are also available which provide physical-modelling guitar amp simulators, elaborate dithering systems for optimising bit reduction (used when converting 20-bit recordings to 16-bit CD masters), vocoder imitation, and even the deliberate addition of noise and crackle to simulate vinyl recordings. These latter devices are fashionable for making new recordings sound like vintage vinyl samples, and include such parameters as record speed, recording age, amount of surface damage and other criteria. Processes such as surround sound, mixing and encoding are also available through the use of plug-ins, enabling a multi-channel audio workstation to handle sophisticated TV and film sound mixing.

The plug-in environment also allows a few more off-the-wall ideas to flourish, such as multiband fuzz boxes, unusual dynamic equalisers with user-adjustable compression curves and frequency points, and various interesting metering systems for viewing stereo image, phase, frequency content and so on. There are also numerous pitch-manipulation packages, including those designed to tune up vocal tracks, stereo width enhancers, 3D sound-positioning algorithms, many types of spectral enhancer and even systems that allow the user to analyse the spectral content of commercial recordings and then automatically EQ recordings to the same spectrum.

At the time of writing the majority of plug-ins are designed to be used within software-recording and -editing environments, but manufacturers of some digital mixers are already adding DSP to their products so that effects and processes from third-party designers can be created within the mixer. This can be only a good thing, as it provide the user with more choice, and may turn out to be a good way of offsetting the shortage of analogue insert points on budget digital mixing consoles.

One clear advantage of using software is that computers are able to provide an excellent graphical interface and so, as well as controls and meters, plug-ins often provide dynamic graphs of criteria such as compressor slopes and EQ curves, and this doesn't take up any extra rack space. However, for most audio software, a monitor of 17 inches or more is recommended.

plug-in automation

It's a well-known fact that some of the parameters of MIDI effects may be automated with MIDI controller data, but many plug-ins may now also be automated, including the popular VST range. While some processes don't lend themselves to automation in any obvious way, effect such as delay, reverb and even guitar-amp simulation can be automated to produce very creative mixes.

software protection

Software piracy is a major problem in some sectors of the industry, and so music software tends to be protected, which can be inconvenient for the legitimate user. However, it prevents unlawful copying of the software, which in the long term should mean better product support and lower prices for the user. Protection comes in several forms, the two most common being hardware keys, or 'dongles', and floppy-disk-limited installs.

Dongles plug in series with a computer port, such as the keyboard buss on a Mac or the serial mouse port on a PC, and without them the software won't run. The user can make multiple backup copies of the software if required, but the copies will only run on a machine that has the correct dongle plugged in. Some manufacturers of plug-ins use a single dongle to authorise their plug-ins, and this usually works with some kind of password system: when you've paid for the plug-in the manufacturer supplies you with a password that effectively upgrades your dongle, allowing you to run the most recent plug-ins.

Copy protection enforced by limited disk installation uses an uncopyable master floppy disk, from which the software is installed. The master disk usually allows the software to be installed twice, and after each install a counter on the floppy is decremented. When there are no more installs left, the only way to persuade the master disk to work again is to de-install the software (again, using the master disk), which increments the counter on the master disk and provides you with one more install. The downside of this system – other than the risk of damaging your master disk – is that, if you need to change computers or reformat your hard drive, you first have to de-install all copy-protected software, and if you have a lot of software this can be a long job. This system has a limited life, however, as floppy disks are gradually being phased out.

A more recent and less intrusive system of copy protection involves using an uncopyable CD-ROM as the master disk. The software is installed from this CD ROM in the normal way, but on random occasions (usually when the program is started up up) the user is asked to insert the master CD-ROM before work can continue.

computing power

The concept of having effects that can run in real time on a host computer with no additional hardware other than a simple soundcard is clearly very attractive, but in order to avoid disappointment you'll need to use the most powerful computer you can afford. Furthermore, you must resign yourself to upgrading your computer every year or two in order to keep pace with newer and more power-hungry software developments. The minimum system requirements stated for software can make it sound like you can get away with using a much less powerful machine, but this is invariably a false impression, especially if you want to run plug-ins. As a rule of thumb, any machine that wasn't state of the art six months ago is to be avoided, as it's probably too slow.

stereo editors

Stereo editors are designed to handle a number of tasks, the most important of which are designing sounds for samplers, editing complete stereo mixes to create new arrangements and assembling final mixes in order to create a finished album master. To perform this successfully, the software must offer the ability to edit precisely and introduce variable crossfades between sections, the ability to create fades, the ability to change levels and the ability to silence unwanted material. Plug-in support is also important, as you may want to equalise or compress the material. In sound design applications, you may also wish to use plug-ins that allow you to process sounds in more abstract ways.

In addition to creating masters for albums, there is also an increasing demand for software that can prepare files for being loaded onto the Internet using compression protocols such as MP3. It's also fairly commonplace for stereo editing packages to support direct CD-R burning facilities so that, once you've mastered your album, you can produce an audio CD directly from it. As long as you have software that offers full 'orange-book' coding (ie it arranges all of the track codes and table of contents in a standard way), you should be able to get a commercial mass-produced CD cut from your CD-R master.

software synths

Synths are becoming increasingly important now that computers are available with adequate CPU power to run them. Computers can handle any type of synthesis, from emulated analogue to FM, sample based, wavetable, additive and even granular. The amount of available polyphony is usually related to the amount of available computer processing power, and such soft synths really come into their own when offering synthesis methods which aren't easily available with existing hardware.

Some driver software is necessary to allow the synths to receive MIDI data and play through your audio hardware, though ASIO support is fairly common. Steinberg's ReWire technology makes the system even more flexible by enabling the output from a virtual synth to be fed through the mixer in the host audio program, which means that it can then be mixed and effected just like any other audio source.

Opcode's OMS (Open MIDI System) software is also commonly used in Mac systems to route MIDI-to-OMS-compatible pieces of software. The main problem with software synthesis is that the latency of the audio hardware may be great enough to prevent the synthesiser from being playable. This sounds serious, but in practice the part can often be recorded with a soundcard synth voice and then played back on the soft synth. The adoption of this method avoids the effects of latency.

samplers

Software samplers are now available which operate much like their hardware counterparts, some using system RAM and others streaming audio directly from the hard drive. Their MIDI control and audio outputs are handled in much the same way as soft synths, so you'll need the right drivers in order to use them in your system. This is definitely a growth area, but SoundFont soundcards developed by Creative Labs have had sampling capability for a long time, and the quality on some of their better-specified cards can be impressive. On cheaper cards, sample RAM must be plugged into the card itself, while on more sophisticated systems it's possible to store sample data on the computer's own system RAM.

In essence, a soundfont is a set of sound samples that can be loaded into a card for playback. Numerous CD-ROMs of soundfonts are commercially available, while the support software that comes with most Soundblaster cards allows .WAV files to be recorded and then edited to create new soundfonts. Although the Soundblaster name is associated with budget games cards, the SoundFont system is actually pretty sophisticated and the quality of some of the commercial sample material available for it is impressive. What's more, SoundFont material tends to be considerably less costly than more professional sample formats.

chapter 5

music computers

In the preceding chapters we've learned that computers can supply us with MIDI sequencing, audio recording, mixing, virtual effects, virtual synths and CD manufacturing, but because of the complexity of the software and the potential for conflicts between software and hardware, setting up a desktop studio isn't always as simple as it might first appear. In this chapter I've put together a few suggestions that will help you to choose the right system, and if you already have one it will help you to use it to its full potential, whether it runs on a Mac or a PC.

If you're planning to buy a PC system but aren't sure which sort to buy, check out the FAQs on the various music web sites, including the extensive FAQ section in the Forum section of the Sound On Sound site at www.sospubs.co.uk. If you know somebody who has a working system and you're prepared to order exactly the same hardware and software, you should be on reasonably safe ground (although parts occasionally change within different models of the same computer).

However, those with limited computer experience should seriously consider buying a pre-configured system from a single vendor.

Choosing a Macintosh isn't as difficult as choosing a PC because there's a limited range of models, as opposed to the infinite permutations of PC configurations. All new Macs use the USB serial interface for the connection of peripherals such as MIDI interfaces, and from the tests I've done so far those with intelligent buffering – such as the EMagic AMT series and the MOTU USB interfaces – provide the best MIDI timing. Newer Macs don't have built-in SCSI facilities, however, so if you want to use the latest and fastest SCSI drives you'll need to fit a SCSI PCI card, just like a PC. You should always contact the software manufacturer's technical support department before buying a SCSI card, or a MIDI interface for that matter, just to ensure that there are no known problems with your selection. If you need fewer audio tracks, a slower (but cheaper) internal EIDE drive may be adequate, but I'd still recommend buying a separate drive rather than using your boot drive. Most Macs have space for a second drive, but if you absolutely must use the same drive for your audio work as the one on which you do everything else, at least create a separate partition for your audio work.

The newer and faster Firewire drives look to be the future of Mac and PC audio storage, but I haven't yet been able to try one.

Note that Macs from the coloured G3 models onwards don't have a floppy drive as standard, though it's possible to buy an external drive that takes regular floppies as well as high-capacity removable disks. Check with your software vendor that this doesn't complicate software installation or the copy-protection system in any way.

recording levels

It's best to optimise the input signal level of any digital recording system at source rather than relying on normalising your system or using software gain control to bring up the level. In most cases, gain control exercised in the software domain simply boosts the low-level signal at the input and brings up any noise by the same amount. You should use the level metering provided in the software to keep peak levels just a few decibels below the point at which clipping occurs for the least distortion and best signal-to-noise ratio.

Regardless of whether your system is capable of 16-, 20- or 24-bit recording, the ultimate sound quality will be defined by the recording made at source. In most cases, the dynamic range of a 16-bit system will exceed the dynamic range of the signal being recorded. For vocals, consider buying a voice channel/pre-amp type of device, which is essentially a good mic amp equipped with EQ and compression. This may also be used when miking other instruments, and many such amps feature an instrumental DI input suitable for bass and clean electric or electroacoustic guitars. Alternatively, you could use the mic pre-amp of a mixer that you know is suitable for recording.

weak links

The fact that computers and recording software packages are such good value for money can lead you into believing that you can make do with using equally cheap components in the rest of the studio, but this simply isn't true, although premium items such as capacitor mics are now much more affordable than they used to be. You should budget for a good microphone, decent cables and – if you don't have a suitable mixer – a mic pre-amp/voice channel. You could get away with using the old dynamic microphone you use at gigs, but in most instances a capacitor mic will provide noticeably better results.

This also applies to your monitor speakers. If they're inaccurate you won't really know what your recording sounds like. Use high-quality monitor loudspeakers on rigid stands and set them up so that you're at the apex of a roughly equilateral triangle, with the monitors pointing directly toward you. You don't need to monitor loudly, but you'll need enough volume to overcome the noise made by the fans and drives in the computer. If you can put your computers in a ventilated cupboard to reduce the noise then so much the better, and lining the cupboard with an inch-thick layer of fireproof furniture foam will also help to damp out noise.

drive maintenance

If you have a separate hard drive for your audio work you'll be able to regularly defragment it, or even reformat it, without disturbing your program files. Defragmenting optimises the rate at which data can be read on and from the drive – a badly-fragmented drive can produce audible glitching and reduce the number of tracks that can be played back simultaneously. Faster drivers can play back more tracks, although very fast drives may need a special, rapid SCSI interface card to make the best of their abilities. Modern hard drives are reasonably reliable, but it's still wise to back up important work to another drive or to another medium, such as CD-ROM. Avoid moving or knocking drives while they are operating, as this can cause serious damage.

When choosing or upgrading a soundcard, try to find one that provides at least four outputs, and a digital S/PDIF Out if you own a DAT machine or MiniDisc recorder. In this way you can use one pair of outputs for tracks that use software-based plug-in effects, while the other outputs can carry tracks that you want to effect with external processors.

effects

Reverb is the most important effect in the studio, and effective reverbs take up a lot of computing capacity. For this reason, it may be worth considering buying a soundcard with its own hardware reverb processing capabilities, or a multi-channel audio interface that allows you to use an external hardware reverb unit.

Unless you are using a fairly sophisticated soundcard with on-board DSP processing, you're likely to experience some latency or delay when monitoring the signal you're recording through the system. ASIO II drivers will minimise this problem in compatible hardware, but it won't cure the problem in all soundcards. One way around this is to use a small mixer, and to monitor the computer's input rather than its output when overdubbing. By monitoring the input source you will avoid problems with latency, but you will also have to monitor without using plug-in software effects.

You will usually need a separate mixer to combine your audio and external synth and sampler signals, and if you hook up a hardware reverb unit to this mixer you'll be able to add reverb to the monitoring as you record. This makes singers feel more comfortable, and can help them to produce a really good vocal performance. You don't need to record the reverb while monitoring; if you leave it until mixing before adding it you keep your options open, and you can then try different settings.

other plug-ins

Not all plug-ins are effects – some are designed to fix problems. The Antares Autotune plug-in is particularly useful, not only in cleaning up vocal pitching but also in tightening up guitar solos, and a cheap VST 'lite' version is available that will work with most MIDI/audio sequencing software. Regular playing will be unaffected as long as the tracking time is set at a slow enough speed, but whenever a note is sustained it will automatically settle on exactly the right pitch. This can be particularly useful for slow pieces that use a lot of string bends.

Every month newer and more sophisticated software plug-ins become available that handle anything from automatic dialogue replacement (for film and TV work) to mastering. The best way of keeping up to speed with what's on the market is reading recording magazines and visiting manufacturers' web sites. However, it's possible to get by with a fairly basic set of plug-ins; for most music work, a good reverb unit and compressor, combined with a delay/echo effect, will satisfy most requirements. Check out the plug-ins that come bundled in with your software before forking out for any new ones, as some of these freebies can work very well.

guitars and computers

One problem that most guitarists come up against is that computer monitors interferes badly with the guitar pickups, resulting in a buzz being picked up on the recording. Some humbucking pickups are reasonably good at rejecting this buzz, as long as the player doesn't sit too close to the monitor while recording, but single-coil pickups affect the sound very badly, especially if overdrive is also used. A cheap way around this problem is to switch off the monitor just before recording and use keyboard commands to start and stop the recording process.

If for some reason you can't switch off the monitor, sit as far away from it as possible when recording and rotate your position to find the null point (the point at which the buzz is least obtrusive). You might also use a noise gate pedal to keep your guitar quiet between phrases. Flat-screen LCD monitors are becoming cheaper, and these take up less space and eliminate the electromagnetic interference generated by the scan coils of CRT monitors. These are good investments if you record a lot of guitar work or you're short on space.

fan and drive noise

Physical noise is also a problem when miking instruments or voices in the same room as the computer. If possible, turn off unnecessary external drives, CD-ROM burners and so on, as these often make more noise than the main computer. Set up your mic (ideally a cardioid model) as far from the computer as possible, and improvise an acoustic screen between the mic and the computer with a duvet or sleeping bag. Also, make sure that the mic is pointing toward an absorbent rather than a reflective surface. Work as close to the mic as possible without compromising the sound, always using a pop shield for vocals. This will be easier if you use a sound-deadening cupboard, as described earlier in this chapter.

waveform editing

Virtually all sequencers capable of recording audio have a Waveform Edit page (although it isn't always called this), where it's possible to highlight and silence selected portions of audio. If background noise is a problem, matters can sometimes be improved by manually silencing the gaps between words and phrases, which doesn't take as long as you think and can really improve the quality of a recording, especially when there are multiple audio tracks. It's a good idea to normalise audio recordings before processing them in order to maximise playback signal-to-noise ratio, although you shouldn't use this as a substitute for arriving at the right recording levels in the first place. Normalising can generally be carried out from within the Waveform Edit page.

Waveform editing can also be used to remove unwanted finger noise from between notes in guitar tracks for those occasions when you end up with a take that's almost perfect, except there's too much squeak or finger noise between notes, or maybe the next string was caught just after a note bend. The silence function will surgically remove these little errors, although if you leave them where they are, and instead reduce them in level by between 6dB and 20dB, you may end up with a more natural sound. In this way you can also silence page turns, coughs and other noises on vocal parts. You can also be very creative, such as adding fade-ins to guitar parts to simulate the action of a swell pedal.

For the greatest possible flexibility when adding effects in the mix, try to record all parts dry – in particular, don't add reverb or delay unless you really have to. Add reverb at the monitoring stage if you need to hear it to create a good performance, but don't record it. In this way you'll be able to edit tracks without cutting holes in the echo or delay effects you've added. Furthermore, if there are any edits that are a bit close for comfort, adding the necessary delay or echo afterwards will help disguise the edit points, making the recording sound quite natural.

computer power

As with any other software, plug-ins always take up a certain amount of the available computing power, so if you want to add the same delay or reverb-based effects to several tracks it's more efficient to use a single plug-in configured as an aux send processor than to use a separate insert plug-in on every track. The aux send controls can generally be used to add different amounts of the same effect to any track, in the same way as a regular mixer, all for the CPU overhead of a single plug-in. You should note, however, that under normal circumstances you can't use the aux send with processes such as EQ, compression or gating – these have to be used with inserts, though you may be able to premix to a group buss and carry out one lot of processing to the sub-mixed tracks rather than having to process each track individually.

Don't try to force your software to do everything for you just because it can; very often you'll find that you can get a better sound with separate devices, and of course they won't burden the processing power of your CPU. You can still compress signals as you record them, even if you don't have a multi-output soundcard, ideally by using a voice-channel-type device as described earlier. This also applies to EQ. Only the best digital EQs sound as natural as even the most basic analogue equalisers.

time and pitch manipulation

There are lots of tricks you can perform with the audio manipulation facilities provided by your sequencer, and many of these extend beyond what you might expect from a simple multi-effects unit. For example, there are very powerful filters that can process any sound to make it appear synthetic, and devices which can distort sound in other interesting ways. Built-in facilities vary from one software package to another, but pitch-changing and time-stretching are supported by most machines. These are invaluable for massaging audio sample loops, but you may also find other tools which provide level-maximising, de-noising and other features. Some of the more processor-intensive processes work off line, so they can be used even on slower machines – you just have to wait a little longer for the results.

Pitch-to-MIDI conversion is also fairly common. This process allows a monophonic recording of an instrument to be analysed in order that a MIDI track mirroring the note and pitch bend information of the original track can be produced. This is useful when you need to configure a MIDI instrument to play along in unison with material from a real instrument that you've just recorded. Some software even offers the ability to quantise audio tracks, which means that the timing of parts such as drums and guitar riffs can be tightened up considerably. In my experience this can work well, as long as you don't process too much material at once and as long as the original audio information isn't too complex. As with so many things, you'll need to experiment to see what works and what doesn't.

keep it clean!

Most computer audio systems run best if you get rid of any superfluous software, such as screen savers and games. You should also make sure that you have no more drivers than you actually need (or extensions, if you're using a Mac) – the cleaner your system the less likely you'll run into problems. Also, check manufacturers' web sites to make sure that you have the most up-to-date drivers or extensions, as improvements are being made all the time. If you must run other software, consider using the dual-boot system described in chapter three, with which two completely different sets of the operating systems, along with the relevant programs, are arranged on two different hard drives. In this way you can start up from your music drive when you're working with audio and from the other drive for everyday work or for playing games.

It's also wise to carry out tests to find out how many tracks and plug-ins your machine can run without running into trouble – try to work with no more than half to two thirds of this amount. Most sequencers are equipped with some kind of CPU activity monitor, but the demands on your CPU aren't constant. Disk drives also slow down as they fragment, so try to allow for this – although you can't be expected to defragment it after recording each track.

computer timing

Problems occasionally arise where the timing of MIDI and/or audio isn't as accurate as it should be. MIDI timing errors (caused by the speed of MIDI data transfer) are small compared to the erratic timing of even a good player, but if you have a composition comprising many MIDI tracks, all of which contain quantised notes at the start of a particular bar, the errors may become noticeable. Fortunately, there are strategies that can be used to improve matters.

You should switch off any type of MIDI message you're not using, so if the track you're recording doesn't require aftertouch it should be switched off at the keyboard. Similarly, if you're using a MIDI guitar controller and the track doesn't require any pitch bend, filter it out or switch to Chromatic mode. Having economised on your data stream in this way, there are also other tricks you can try. All MIDI instruments take a short time to respond to incoming MIDI data, which can exaggerate any delays that occur normally. If you have an instrument that you know is relatively slow, try applying a negative delay to the track in your sequencer's playback parameter section so that the MIDI data arrives a few milliseconds before the beat. This will speed up the response of the synth and also avoid the bottleneck of too many notes trying to squeeze out on one quantise segment. A similar trick can be achieved with slow attack sounds, such as strings – it's possible to advance most slow string or pad sounds by several milliseconds before any timing differences can be heard. Indeed, it's always best to avoid having too many quantised notes falling at the same time, so if you can leave something unquantised then so much the better.

Back in the old days, when the Atari ST was state-of-the-art technology, it was said that you should put drums and other parts with critical timing on the lowest-numbered tracks, as MIDI channels with low numbers had timing priority. Today's sequencers are able to move tracks, but it's still likely that data will be processed in order of MIDI channel, so it's a good idea to put all parts for which timing is critical on the first few channels. If none of this fixes your problems, and you're using a MIDI interface that's part of a cheap soundcard, you should consider buying a more sophisticated MIDI interface. Before spending any more money, however, see if you can obtain more recent drivers from your card manufacturer, as these can sometimes make a big difference to a performance.

Using a multiport MIDI interface may also tighten up timing, although much depends on the speed at which the computer communicates with the interface. If you're using multitimbral synths with a multiport interface, try to reserve a separate port for each one, even if you're not using all 16 channels.

The newer EMagic and MOTU interfacing systems tighten up timing even further by sending data to the MIDI interface a short while before it is needed, where it's held in a memory buffer. The data is then clocked out of all ports simultaneously at the appropriate time, providing the best resolution MIDI has to offer.

lightening the load

Your MIDI and audio timing can be optimised by ensuring that your computer isn't carrying out any unnecessary tasks in the background. Scrolling screen displays usually take up more processing power than those that jump when the cursor gets to the end of the screen, so try turning off the scrolling function if you think you're pushing your computer's capabilities. Even better, reduce the magnification of the song's display so that it all fits into a single page before you play it back – in this way there's no scrolling or screen redraw.

Mac users should also try using the Extensions Manager control panel to disable any system extensions that aren't necessary, and screen savers are definitely something to avoid. Configuring the monitor resolution to 256 colours also reduces the processing burden.

audio timing

Most people can get by with the resolution of MIDI, but if audio material refuses to stay in time with the MIDI tracks it can be extremely frustrating. There are several reasons this can happen. Latency is something that many users have to accept when monitoring while recording, but if it's too bad it can be improved if the input signal is monitored over a hardware mixer. When the audio material is transferred onto your computer's hard drive, however, playback timing can still wander around to an unacceptable degree if your computer is short of RAM, if it's slower than at least twice what the manufacturers claim as a minimum specification, or if the software drivers are not up to date. This latter consideration is important, because a poorly-written driver may allow the playback latency to waver, which has the effect of causing the audio timing to drift. You should also check out the pages of driver settings, adjusting the amount of RAM buffering and playback delay settings until your system behaves properly. Fortunately, many soundcard manufacturers recommended settings to ensure compatibility with the more common software packages.

Check that you're not asking the computer to start playing the audio material on the first beat of a sequence. When the Start button is pressed on a sequencer a certain amount of behind-the-scenes activity (buffer filling, etc) takes place before it's possible for the audio to start playing back. If the audio material starts on the first beat of the song, give the sequencer time to prepare for playback by inserting a couple of empty bars between the time when the count-in stops and the song starts.

audio and clocks

When audio material is recorded onto a computer, the data is usually timed by a crystal clock fitted to the soundcard; however, although crystal clocks are very stable, they don't all run at exactly the same speed as each other, which means that, if you have a system with two or more soundcards, you have to be careful when recording with one soundcard and playing back with another, as the playback speed on both cards may be slightly different. This situation should be avoided if each track is replayed with the card that recorded it, but things can still go wrong in a system if you try to sync all of your audio to an external digital timing. Again, the playback speed may drift slightly if the external clock doesn't run at exactly the same speed as the clocks on your soundcards, and on long audio tracks the drift becomes more pronounced the further the track progresses. If you intend to synchronise all of your cards on playback, sync'ing them while you're recording as well will lessen the chances of drift.

sync

What happens when your audio is stable but you decide to sync the sequencer to a less-than-perfectly-stable outside source, such as a tape recorder? If the master device runs a little slow the MIDI sequence tempo will drop to match it, but the audio may then carry on playing at its original rate, causing the MIDI and audio material to drift apart. The better sequencers have something called continuous audio resync, which changes the audio clock speed to match that of the time code produced by the master machine, but not all machines are equipped with this facility.

If you're using a number of soundcards in order to gain more individual audio outputs, it's also unwise to split stereo pairs of signals between two cards because even the slightest difference in timing will cause an unpleasant flanging effect. Wherever possible, record stereo material as a stereo audio file – in this way the two halves can't drift.

solutions

If the stability of your audio timing is still inadequate, despite your best endeavours, one of the most effective solutions to this particular problem is to divide long audio tracks into sections of just a few bars long. Each section will trigger independently so that, although there may still be a small amount of drift within each section, the effect won't be cumulative.

Cubase VST provides a priority setting in its System Setup page, which defaults to 'normal', giving equal priority to both audio and MIDI. If you work mainly with audio, however, you can change this to 'high' or 'highest', giving priority to audio data processing. If you work mainly with MIDI, on the other hand, setting this to 'low' will ensure that MIDI has priority. With VST, it's also important to have the correct setting for system pre-roll (located in the Sync menu). Normally this should be set to the same value as the soundcard's latency.

When creating audio loops within a sequencer, much depends on how slick the sequencer is at retriggering the same piece of audio. If slight timing discrepancies arise when the sequencer jumps back to the start of the audio segment, you may be able to make a small tempo change of usually a very small fraction of a beat per minute to compensate. If you can't find a satisfactory solution, however, you should perhaps consider entrusting your drum loops to an external sampler.

Ultimately, a great deal depends on the quality of the computer. It should obviously be capable of processing MIDI and audio, but we also expect them to be able to deal with mixing, EQ, VST real-time effects and even virtual synthesis. Unless you have the most powerful computer, you may find that many problems are simply caused by having an under-powered system. Manufacturers also confuse the issue by quoting hopelessly inadequate minimum specifications on software packages.

To get the best out of your system, make sure that you have plenty of memory available – ideally double that of the minimum specified, or more – and take some time to check manufacturers' web sites to download the latest drivers and setup information for your hardware. If support helplines can't help you, user groups are probably the best place to start looking for answers to any problems you still can't resolve.

creating an album

You've recorded all of your MIDI tracks, recorded your audio tracks and you've set up a mix that sounds great. So now what? Ultimately you need to end up with a stereo master recording, and how you proceed from this point depends on the type of system you're using. If you have an external DAT or MiniDisc recorder you can mix to this, either straight from your soundcard output or with an external mixer. The external mixer provides more flexibility if used in conjunction with a multi-output soundcard or if you have hardware synths, but if you're working with a soundcard that provides a single stereo mix of audio and MIDI tracks then there's little advantage to be had in using a mixer. In fact, best results can be obtained by feeding the digital output from your soundcard (if you have one) directly into your digital recorder's digital input. Once your mix is on DAT or MiniDisc you will then be able to feed it back into the computer when you want to compile your album.

If you don't have a digital recorder, you'll need to create your master mix as a stereo sound file on the computer and then work on this with your editing software. Different soundcards may handle this procedure in slightly different ways, so refer to your soundcard manual to find out the best way to do this. If you have recorded the original material with a bit depth of more than 16 bits, it should be re-recorded at 16-bit resolution at this stage.

mastering

Once you have a collection of mixed songs stored as stereo sound files on your hard drive, you may want to put them together to make an album, and with the cheapness of CD-R burners and CD-R discs, why not? However, before burning a CD there may be a few mastering tricks you can employ to make the tracks sound even better. Moreover, you may need to tweak tracks that were recorded or mixed at different times so that they sit together comfortably, and this may require both level and tonal adjustment. Although professional mastering engineers use a lot of esoteric equipment to achieve this, there's no reason why you shouldn't get impressive results with software plug-ins. The most important tool is the ear of the person doing the job.

I'd recommend a plug-in tool kit comprising, as a minimum, a good parametric equaliser and a compressor/limiter. Enhancer-type plug-ins can also be used as de-noising devices if your finished mix has more hiss than you'd like. You'll also need an accurate monitoring environment, which means using hi-fi speakers rather than plastic computer speakers with a bass speaker the size of a shoebox stuck under the desk.

Most mistakes are the result of over-processing, and the old adage 'if it ain't broke, don't fix it' holds true with mastering. Don't feel that you have to process music just because you can, or you might find that your mastered sounds are worse than your original material. Here are a few tips to help you make the best of your recordings.

The endings of fadeouts should be handled with the computer editor. Not only does the computer provide more control but it will also fade out any background noise along with the music so that the song ends in perfect silence. You should also silence any background noise that occurs just before the recording so that your track also starts from complete silence. Endings should be faded out rather than silenced in order to mimic the natural decay exhibited by most instruments. Start to fade when the last note or beat has decayed to around 5% of its maximum level, and make it around one second long so that the song finishes in silence. Including around half a second of silence at the start of each song will mean that slow CD players won't miss the start of the song.

Once you've decided on a running order for the tracks you'll need to match up levels, but this doesn't mean simply making everything the same level. If you do this, more restrained material, such as ballads, will seem very loud when compared to stronger songs. The vocal level will often be the best guide to how well songs are matched, but your ears are the best judges. Close your eyes and try to hear if the songs sit comfortably together, tweaking levels until they sound as natural as possible.

mastering EQ

If the tracks were recorded at different times or in different studios, changing levels may not be enough. A little EQ will often improve matters, although a good parametric EQ will be required to avoid making matters worse. Listen to the bass ends of all songs to determine how they differ, and use EQ to try and even things out. For example, one song might have all of its bass energy bunched up at around 80Hz or 90Hz, while another might have an extended deep bass dropping right down to 40Hz or below, and by rolling off the sub-bass and peaking up the 80Hz area slightly you may be able to focus the bass end. Also, the track with the bunched-up bass could be treated by adding a gentle boost at 40Hz, combined with a little cut at around 120Hz. All equalisers behave differently, so you'll need to experiment.

To make a track sound louder when it's already peaking close to digital full scale, use a digital limiter such as the excellent Waves L1 or Logic Audio's Energizer. The overall level can usually be increased by at least 6dB before it becomes clear that the peaks have been processed.

gentle compression

Overall compression can also add energy to a mix and help to even out the material, but it isn't mandatory: music needs some light and shade in order to provide dynamics. A compressor will often slightly change the apparent balance of a mix, so you may need to use it in combination with EQ. If the EQ is applied before the compressor then the boosted frequencies will be compressed the most, while applying it after the compressor will allow you to equalise the compressed sound without affecting the operation of the compressor. The best arrangement to choose will depends on the material you're treating, so you should try both. A split band compressor or dynamic equaliser will provide you with more scope to change the spectral balance of a mix, but it takes a little practice to use these devices so that you feel like you're controlling them, rather than vice versa. I find that the best results are achieved by using compression ratios below 1.5:1, and with the threshold set at between -10dB and -30dB.

After applying compression, listen to the finished master all the way through over a pair of headphones, which will show up small glitches and noises that loudspeakers may mask – digital clicks can appear in even the best systems.

de-noising

Digital de-noising programs can't work miracles – even the best systems produce side-effects if pushed too far. The simpler systems are effectively multiband expanders on which the threshold of each band is determined after analysing a section of noise from between tracks. It's therefore best not to clean up original masters before they're edited, or there may be no noise samples left from which to work. You should be able to achieve a few decibels of noise reduction before the side-effects kick in – as low-level signals open and close the expanders in the various bands, the background noise is modulated in a way that can only be described as chirping. This chirping become worse the more noise reduction you try to achieve, so it's best to use as little as possible.

track editing

If you need to make edits within individual tracks when compiling a version from all of the best sections of several mixes or recordings, try to make joins just before or just after a drum beat so that any discontinuities are masked by the beat. However, if you have to use a crossfade edit to smooth over a transition, try to avoid including a drumbeat in the crossfade zone or you may hear a phasing effect when the beats overlap. Crossfades should be as short as possible in order to avoid producing a double-tracked effect during the fade zone – as little as 10-30ms is enough to avoid producing a click. Once edited, resave the track as a new sound file.

making a CD

Most CD burners come bundled with software suitable for making audio CDs, but if you wish to use the CD as the master for pressing commercial CDs then you will need to choose software that offers 'red-book' PQ (Pause and Cue) coding so that the disc you burn has the same data format as a commercial CD. The disc must be written in 'disc at once' mode, rather than a track at a time, in order to avoid introducing errors between tracks. Check with your CD manufacturer to confirm that their device can work from CD-R as a master, and take note of any special requirements it may have.

Virtually all CD-burning software includes a playlist feature, on which individual song files (or sometimes regions of files) are added into the playlist, and the gap between the tracks can then be determined by the user. The default value is generally around two seconds, but this can be changed if required. Figure 6.1 shows the playlist from Adaptec's Jam program for the Macintosh, which is pretty typical for such software.

When you're deciding on the space between tracks on an album, listen to how the first track ends and how the second one starts. Gaps are rarely shorter than two seconds, but if the starts and ends of tracks are very abrupt you may need to leave up to four seconds between tracks. Use the pre-roll feature of your digital editor to listen to the transition so that you can judge when the next track should start.

When you're ready to burn the CD, load in a blank CD-R, and avoid touching the flat surface because dirt or fingerprints will cause errors in the writing process. You should also resist the temptation to use cheap, unbranded discs, as some of these are prone to high rates of error, short storage lives or both. It's also a good idea to run the software in Test mode to check that the burn will work, without introducing errors, at the write speed you've chosen. If an error creeps in during a real burn you'll end up with an expensive coaster!

the Internet

Making your audio files available on an Internet site is a good way of publicising your music, and there are two main ways of doing this. In both cases the amount of audio data needs to be reduced, because straight .WAV files are very large and take forever to download. One approach is to use the popular MP3 data-compression format, which reduces audio files so that they are less than a tenth of the size of the original .WAV file and yet

	Pause	Start	Title	Length	Gain	Xfade	CP PE	ISRC
▷ 4	00:03:00	10:44:17	Region 12	03:44:03	2.3	][	■ □	
▷ 5	00:02:00	14:30:20	Region 26	04:48:12	0.0	][	■ □	
▷ 6	00:03:00	19:21:32	Region 30	03:49:32	0.0	][	■ □	
▷ 7	00:03:00	23:13:64	Region 42 Revised	03:37:64	0.0	][	■ □	
▷ 8	00:03:00	26:54:53	When all said and don...	02:49:38	-2.0	][	■ □	
▷ 9	00:03:00	29:47:16	Never Fly Fixed	05:09:23	-8.0	][	■ □	
▷ 10	00:03:00	34:59:39	New Day Fixed	04:02:19	-1.0	][	■ □	
▷ 11	00:03:00	39:04:58	First Time Love Fixed	03:33:14	0.0	][	■ □	
▷ 12	00:03:00	42:40:72	Celebrate Fixed	03:53:11	0.0	][	■ □	
▷ 13	00:02:00	46:36:08	Everybody Knows Fixed	04:07:22	0.0	][	■ □	
▷ 14	00:03:00	50:46:30	Region 13	03:06:28	-4.0	][	■ □	
▷ 15	00:01:00	53:53:58	Region 11	02:32:28	0.0	][	■ □	
▷ 16	00:03:00	56:29:11	Region 10	03:46:10	-2.0	][	■ □	

Figure 6.1: CD burning playlist

retain almost all of the original subjective audio quality.
MP3 files can be downloaded like any other file and then
either played back by the computer or a hardware MP3
player. MP3 is the most popular format for selling audio
material over the Internet, but even so one minute of
stereo audio will still require something like 1Mb of data.

The other method is to use a lo-fi streaming format, such
as RealAudio. These files are much more heavily
compressed than MP3, and sound noticeably
compromised, but they're still of sufficient quality to
allow listeners to tell whether they like the music or not.
The advantage of using a streaming file is that, once a
small part of it has been downloaded, that part of the file
can be played as the rest downloads – you don't have to
wait for the whole thing to be downloaded, as you do
with MP3. This makes it more suitable for those casually
browsing record catalogues or musicians' web sites.

You'll need to buy encoding software to turn .WAV or SDII
files into MP3 files or a streaming format like RealAudio
(although MP3 encoding is now included in some editing
packages), but the recipient can usually download a free
program from the software vendor to play them. For this
reason, you should always include a link in your site so
that visitors can easily obtain this software. MP3 playback
is often supported via plug-ins for existing browsers.

common cable connections

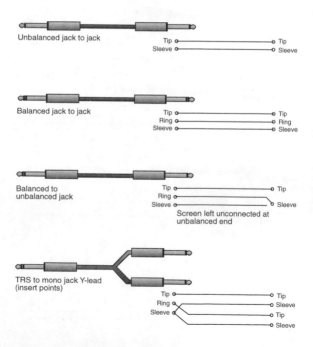

Unbalanced jack to jack

Tip o————————o Tip
Sleeve o————————o Sleeve

Balanced jack to jack

Tip o————————o Tip
Ring o————————o Ring
Sleeve o————————o Sleeve

Balanced to
unbalanced jack

Tip o————————o Tip
Ring o———————
Sleeve o————————o Sleeve
Screen left unconnected at
unbalanced end

TRS to mono jack Y-lead
(insert points)

Tip o————————o Tip
Ring o———————o Sleeve
Sleeve o———————o Tip
————————o Sleeve

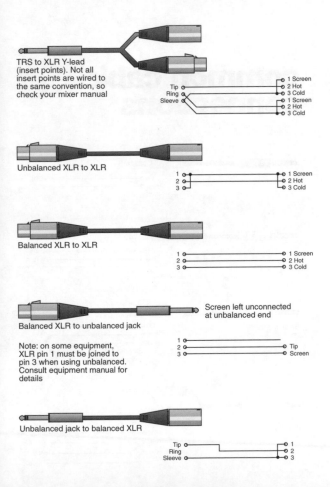

TRS to XLR Y-lead
(insert points). Not all
insert points are wired to
the same convention, so
check your mixer manual

Tip
Ring
Sleeve

1 Screen
2 Hot
3 Cold
1 Screen
2 Hot
3 Cold

Unbalanced XLR to XLR

1
2
3

1 Screen
2 Hot
3 Cold

Balanced XLR to XLR

1
2
3

1 Screen
2 Hot
3 Cold

Balanced XLR to unbalanced jack

Screen left unconnected
at unbalanced end

Note: on some equipment,
XLR pin 1 must be joined to
pin 3 when using unbalanced.
Consult equipment manual for
details

1
2
3

Tip
Screen

Unbalanced jack to balanced XLR

Tip
Ring
Sleeve

1
2
3

glossary

active
Circuit containing transistors, ICs, tubes and other devices that require power to operate and are capable of amplification.

A/D converter
Circuit for converting analogue waveforms into a series of values represented by binary numbers. The more bits a converter has the greater the resolution of the sampling process. Current effects units are generally 16 bits or more, with the better models being either 20- or 24-bit.

AFL
After-Fade Listen, a system used within mixing consoles to allow specific signals to be monitored at the level set by their fader or level control knob. Aux sends are generally monitored AFL rather than PFL so that the actual signal being fed to an effects unit can be monitored.

aftertouch
Means of generating a control signal based on how much pressure is applied to the keys of a MIDI keyboard.

algorithm
Computer program designed to perform a specific task. All digital effects are based on algorithms.

aliasing
When an analogue signal is sampled for conversion into a

digital data stream, the sampling frequency must be at least twice that of the highest frequency component of the input signal. If this rule is disobeyed, the sampling process becomes ambiguous, as there are insufficient points to define each waveform cycle, resulting in enharmonic sum and difference frequencies being added to the audible signal.

ambience
The result of sound reflections in a confined space being added to the original sound. Ambience may also be created electronically by some digital reverb units.

amplifier
Device that increases the level of an electrical signal.

amplitude
Another word for level. Refers to sound or electrical signal.

analogue
Circuitry that uses a continually-changing voltage or current to represent a signal. The term originates from the fact that the electrical signal is analogous to the original signal.

anti-aliasing filter
Filter used to limit the frequency range of an analogue signal prior to A/D conversion so that the maximum frequency does not exceed half the sampling rate.

attack
Time taken for a sound to achieve maximum amplitude.

attenuate
To make lower in level.

audio frequency
Signals in the human audio range, nominally 20Hz-20kHz.

aux

Control on a mixing console designed to route a portion of the channel signal to effects or cue mix outputs (see Aux Send).

aux return
Mixer inputs used to add effects to the mix.

aux send
Physical output from a mixer aux send buss.

balance
This word has several meanings in recording. It may refer to the relative levels of the left and right channels of a stereo recording, or it may be used to describe the relative levels of the various instruments and voices within a mix.

balanced wiring
Wiring system which uses two out-of-phase conductors and a common screen to reduce the effect of interference.

bandwidth
Means of specifying the range of frequencies passed by an electronic circuit such as an amplifier, mixer or filter. The frequency range is usually measured at the points where the level drops by 3dB relative to the maximum.

binary
Counting system based on only two numbers: one and zero.

boost/cut control
Single control which allows the range of frequencies passing through a filter to be either amplified or attenuated. The centre position is usually the 'flat' or 'no effect' position.

bouncing
Process of mixing two or more recorded tracks together and re-recording these onto another track.

buffer

Circuit which isolates the output of a source device from loading effects due to the input impedance of the destination device.

buffer memory
Temporary RAM memory used in some computer operations, sometimes to prevent a break in the data stream when the computer is interrupted to perform another task.

buss
Common electrical signal path along which signals may travel. In a mixer, there are several busses carrying the stereo mix, the groups, the PFL signal, the aux sends and so on. Power supplies are also fed along busses.

cardioid
Literally 'heart shaped'. Describes the polar response of a unidirectional microphone.

channel
In the context of MIDI, Channel refers to one of 16 possible data channels over which MIDI data may be sent.

channel
In the context of mixing consoles, a channel is a single strip of controls relating to one input.

chorus
Effect created by doubling a signal and adding delay and pitch modulation.

chromatic
Describes a scale of pitches rising in steps of one semitone.

click track
Metronome pulse which helps musicians to keep time.

clipping
Severe form of distortion which occurs when a signal attempts

to exceed the maximum level which the equipment can handle.

compressor
Device which reduces the dynamic range of audio signals by reducing the level of high signals or by increasing the level of low signals.

conductor
Material that provides low resistance for electrical current.

console
Alternative term for mixer.

cut-and-paste editing
Copying or moving parts of a recording to different locations.

cutoff frequency
Frequency above or below which attenuation begins in a filter circuit.

cycle
One complete vibration of a sound source or its electrical equivalent. One cycle per second is expressed as one Hertz (Hz).

daisy chain
Term used to describe serial electrical connection between devices or modules.

damping
Refers to the rate at which reverberant energy is absorbed by the various surfaces in an acoustic environment.

DAT
Digital Audio Tape. The most commonly-used DAT machines are more correctly known as R-DATs because they use a rotating head similar to that in a video recorder. Digital recorders using fixed or stationary heads (such as DCC) are known as S-DAT machines.

data compression
System for reducing the amount of data stored by a digital system. Most audio data compression systems are known as lossy systems, as some of the original signal is discarded in accordance with psychoacoustic principles designed to ensure that only components which cannot be heard are lost.

dB
Decibel. Unit used to express the relative levels of two electrical voltages, powers or sounds.

DDL
Digital Delay Line.

decay
Progressive reduction in amplitude of a sound or electrical signal over time.

defragmentation
Process of rearranging the files on a hard disk so that all of the files are as contiguous as possible, and that the remaining free space is also contiguous.

DI
Direct Inject, in which a signal is plugged directly into an audio chain without the aid of a microphone. A DI box is a device for matching the signal-level impedance of a source to a tape machine or mixer input.

digital
Electronic system which represents data and signals in the form of codes comprising ones and zeros.

disk
Abbreviation of diskette, but now used to describe computer floppy, hard and removable disks (see Floppy Disk).

dither

System of adding low-level noise to a digitised audio signal in a way which extends low-level resolution at the expense of a slight deterioration in noise performance.

DMA
Direct Memory Access. Part of a computer operating system that allows peripheral devices to communicate directly with the memory without going via the CPU (Central Processing Unit).

driver
Piece of software that handles communications between the main program and a hardware peripheral, such as a soundcard, printer or scanner.

drum pad
Synthetic playing surface which produces electronic trigger signals in response to being hit with drumsticks.

dry
Signal to which no effects have been added. Conversely, a sound which has been treated with an effect, such as reverberation, is referred to as wet.

DSP
Digital Signal Processor. Microchip designed to processes digital signals.

dubbing
Adding further material to an existing recording. Also known as overdubbing.

dynamic microphone
Type of mic that works on the electric generator principle, where a diaphragm moves a coil of wire within a magnetic field.

dynamic range
Range in decibels between the highest signal that can be handled by a piece of equipment and the level at which small

signals disappear into the noise floor.

dynamics
Method of describing relative levels within a piece of music.

early reflections
First sound reflections from walls, floors and ceilings following a sound created in an acoustically reflective environment.

effects return
Additional mixer input designed to accommodate the output from an effects unit.

effects unit
Device for treating an audio signal in order to change it in some creative way. Effects often involve the use of delay circuits, and include such treatments as reverb and echo.

enhancer
Device which brightens audio material using techniques like dynamic equalisation, phase shifting and harmonic generation.

envelope
How the level of a sound or signal varies over time.

equaliser
Device which cuts or boosts parts of the audio spectrum.

exciter
Enhancer that synthesises new high-frequency harmonics.

expander
Device designed to decrease the level of low-level signals and increase the level of high-level signals, thus increasing the dynamic range of the signal.

fader
Sliding control used in mixers and other processors.

filter
Electronic circuit designed to emphasise or attenuate a specific range of frequencies.

flanging
Modulated delay using feedback to create a sweeping sound.

floppy disk
Computer disk that uses a flexible magnetic medium encased in a protective plastic sleeve.

foldback
System for feeding one or more mixes to performers for use while recording and overdubbing. Also known as a cue mix.

fragmentation
Process where the storing and erasing of files splits up the space on a disk drive into small sections (see Defragmentation).

frequency
Indication of how many cycles of a repetitive waveform occur in one second. A waveform which has a repetition cycle of once per second has a frequency of 1Hz.

frequency response
Measurement of the frequency range that can be handled by a specific piece of electrical equipment or loudspeaker.

gain
Amount by which a circuit amplifies a signal.

gate
Electrical signal that is generated whenever a key is depressed on an electronic keyboard. This is used to trigger envelope generators and other events that need to be synchronised to key action. Also refers to an electronic device designed to mute low-level signals, thus improving the noise performance during pauses in the wanted material.

graphic equaliser

Equaliser on which narrow segments of the audio spectrum are controlled by individual cut/boost faders. So called because the fader positions provide a graphic representation of the EQ curve.

group

Collection of signals within a mixer that are mixed and then routed through a separate fader to provide overall control.

hard disk

High-capacity computer storage device based on a rotating rigid disk with a magnetic coating.

harmonic

High-frequency component of a complex waveform.

Hz

Shorthand for Hertz, the unit of frequency.

impedance

Can be visualised as the AC resistance of a circuit which contains both resistive and reactive components.

insert point

Connector that allows an external processor to be patched into a signal path so that the signal then flows through the processor.

I/O

The part of a system that handles inputs and outputs, usually in the digital domain.

jack

Common audio connector, either mono (TS) or stereo (TRS).

limiter

Device that controls the gain of a signal so as to prevent it from ever exceeding a preset level. A limiter is essentially a fast-acting compressor with an infinite compression ratio.

linear
Device where the output is a direct multiple of the input.

line level
Mixers and signal processors tend to work at a standard signal level known as line level. In practice there are several different standard line levels, but all are in the order of a few volts.

low-frequency oscillator (LFO)
Oscillator used as a modulation source, usually below 20Hz. The most common LFO waveshape is the sine wave, though there is often a choice of sine, square, triangular and sawtooth waveforms.

MDM
Modular Digital Multitrack. A digital recorder that can be used in multiples to provide a greater number of synchronised tracks than a single machine.

mic level
Low-level signal generated by a microphone. This must be amplified many times to increase it to line level.

MIDI
Musical Instrument Digital Interface.

MIDI bank change
Type of controller message used to select alternate banks of MIDI programs where access to more than 128 programs is required.

MIDI controller
Term used to describe the physical interface by which the musician plays the MIDI synthesiser or other sound generator.

(standard) MIDI file
Standard file format for storing song data recorded on a MIDI sequencer in such as way as to allow it to be read by other makes or models of MIDI sequencer.

MIDI in
The socket used to receive information from a master controller or from the MIDI Thru socket of a slave unit.

MIDI program change
Type of MIDI message used to change sound patches on a remote module or the effects patch on a MIDI effects unit.

MIDI thru
Socket on a slave unit used to feed the MIDI In socket of the next unit in line.

MIDI thru box
Device which splits the MIDI Out signal of a master instrument or sequencer to avoid daisy chaining.

monitor
Reference loudspeaker used for mixing. Also refers to a computer's VDU.

monitoring
Action of listening to a mix or a specific audio signal.

monophonic
One note at a time.

multitimbral module
MIDI sound source capable of producing several different sounds at the same time and controlled on different MIDI channels.

multitrack
Device capable of recording several 'parallel' parts or tracks which may then be mixed or re-recorded independently.

noise reduction
System for reducing analogue tape noise or for reducing the level of hiss present in a recording.

normalise

A socket is said to be normalised when it is wired such that the original signal path is maintained, unless a plug is inserted into the socket. The most common examples of normalised connectors are the insert points on a mixing console.

octave

The shift in range of a pitch when its frequency is doubled.

off-line

Process carried out while a recording is not playing. For example, some computer-based processes have to be carried out off-line as the computer isn't fast enough to carry out the process in real time.

oscillator

Circuit designed to generate a periodic electrical waveform.

overdub

To add another part to a multitrack recording or to replace one of the existing parts (see Dubbing).

pan pot

Control enabling the user of a mixer to move the signal to any point in the stereo soundstage by varying the relative levels fed to the left and right stereo outputs.

parallel

Method of connecting two or more circuits together so that their inputs and outputs are all connected together.

parametric EQ

Equaliser with separate controls for frequency, bandwidth and cut/boost.

patch

Alternative term for program. Referring to a single programmed sound within a synthesiser that can be called up using program-change commands. MIDI effects units and samplers also have patches.

patch bay
System of panel-mounted connectors used to bring inputs and outputs to a central point from where they can be routed using plug-in patch cords.

PFL
Pre-Fade Listen. A system used within a mixing console to allow the operator to listen in on a selected signal, regardless of the position of the fader controlling that signal.

phase
Timing difference between two electrical waveforms expressed in degrees where 360° corresponds to a delay of one cycle.

phaser
Effect which combines a signal with a phase-shifted version of itself to produce creative filtering effects. Most phasers are controlled by means of an LFO.

phono plug
Hi-fi connector developed by RCA and used extensively on semi-pro, unbalanced recording equipment.

pickup
Part of a guitar that converts string vibrations to electrical signals.

pitch bend
Control message designed to produce a change in pitch in response to the movement of a pitch-bend wheel. Pitch-bend data can be recorded and edited, just like other MIDI controller data, although it isn't part of the controller message group.

pitch shifter
Device for changing the pitch of an audio signal without changing its duration.

polyphony

An instrument's ability to play two or more notes simultaneously. An instrument which can play only one note at a time is described as monophonic.

poly mode

The most common MIDI mode, which allows any instrument to respond to multiple simultaneous notes transmitted on a single MIDI channel.

portamento

Gliding effect that allows a sound to change pitch gradually when a new key is pressed or MIDI note sent.

post-fade

Aux signal taken from after the channel fader so that the aux send level follows any channel fader changes. Normally used for feeding effects devices.

PQ coding

Process for adding pause, cue and other subcode information to a digital master tape in preparation for CD manufacture.

pre-fade

Aux signal taken from before the channel fader so that the channel fader has no effect on the aux send level. Normally used for creating foldback or cue mixes.

processor

Device designed to treat an audio signal by changing its dynamics or frequency content. Examples of processors include compressors, gates and equalisers.

punch-in

Action of placing an already recorded track into record at the correct time during playback so that the existing material may be extended or replaced.

punch-out
Action of switching a tape machine (or other recording device) out of record after executing a punch in.

Q
Measurement of the resonant properties of a filter. The higher the Q, the more resonant the filter and the narrower the range of frequencies that are allowed to pass.

quantising
Means of moving notes recorded in a MIDI sequencer so that they line up with user defined subdivisions of a musical bar – 16s, for example. May be used to correct timing errors, but over-quantising can remove the human feel from a performance.

RAM
Random Access Memory. This is a type of memory used by computers for the temporary storage of programs and data, and all data is lost when the power is turned off. For that reason, work needs to be saved to disk if it is not to be lost.

R-DAT
Digital tape machine using a rotating head system.

real time
Audio process that can be carried out as the signal is being recorded or played back. The opposite is off-line, where the signal is processed in non-real time.

release
Time taken for a level or gain to return to normal. Often used to describe the rate at which a synthesised sound reduces in level after a key has been released.

resolution
Accuracy with which an analogue signal is represented by a digitising system. The more bits are used, the more accurately the amplitude of each sample can be measured, but there are

other elements of converter design that also affect accuracy. High conversion accuracy is known as high resolution.

resonance
Same as Q.

reverb
Acoustic ambience created by multiple reflections in a confined space.

ROM
Abbreviation for Read-Only Memory. This is a permanent and non-volatile type of memory containing data that can't be changed. Operating systems are often stored on ROM as the memory remains intact when the power is switched off.

sample
Process carried out by an A/D converter where the instantaneous amplitude of a signal is measured many times per second (44.1kHz in the case of CD). Also refers to the digitised sound used as a musical sound source in a sampler or additive synthesiser.

sample rate
Number of times which an A/D converter samples the incoming waveform each second.

SCSI
(Pronounced 'skuzzi'.) Small Computer System Interface. An interfacing system for using hard drives, scanners, CD-ROM drives and similar peripherals with a computer. Each SCSI device has its own ID number and no two SCSI devices in the same chain must be set to the same number. The last device in the chain should be terminated either via an internal terminator or via a plug-in terminator fitted to a SCSI socket.

sequencer
Device for recording and replaying MIDI data, usually in a

multitrack format, allowing complex compositions to be built up a part at a time.

signal-to-noise ratio
Ratio of maximum signal level to the residual noise, expressed in decibels.

sub-bass
Frequencies below the range of typical monitor speakers. Some define sub-bass as frequencies that can be felt rather than heard.

subcode
Hidden data within the CD and DAT format that includes such information as the absolute time location, number of tracks, total running time and so on.

sync
System for making two or more pieces of equipment run in synchronism with each other.

synthesiser
Electronic musical instrument designed to create a wide range of sounds, both imitative and abstract.

tempo
Speed of a piece of music, measured here in beats per minute.

thru
MIDI connector which passes on the signal received at the MIDI In socket.

timbre
Tonal 'colour' of a sound.

track
This term dates back to multitrack tape, on which the tracks are physical stripes of recorded material located side by side along the length of the tape.

transpose

To shift a musical signal by a fixed number of semitones.

TRS jack

Stereo-type jack with tip, ring and sleeve connections.

unbalanced

Two-wire electrical signal connection where the inner (hot or positive) conductor is usually surrounded by the cold (negative) conductor, forming a screen against interference.

velocity

The rate at which a key is depressed. This may be used to control loudness (to simulate the response of instruments such as pianos) or other parameters on later synthesisers.

vibrato

Pitch modulation using an LFO to modulate a VCO.

voice

Capacity of a synthesiser to play a single musical note. An instrument capable of playing 16 simultaneous notes is said to be a 16-voice instrument.

XLR

Type of connector commonly used to carry balanced audio signals, including the feeds from microphones.

Y-lead

Lead split so that one source can feed two destinations. Y-leads may also be used in console insert points, when a stereo jack plug at one end of the lead is split into two monos at the other.